Early experiences

A Unit for teachers

D0841824

Published for the Schools Council by
Macdonald Educational, London and Milwaukee

First published in Great Britain 1972 by
Macdonald Educational Ltd
Holywell House, Worship Street
London EC2A 2EN

Macdonald-Raintree Inc.
205 W. Highland Avenue
Milwaukee, Wisconsin 53203

Reprinted 1973 (with amendments), 1974, 1976 (with amendments), 1977, 1979

ISBN 0 356 04005 4

Library of Congress Catalog Card Number 77-82994

The chief author of this book is:

Roy Richards

The other members of the Science 5/13 team are:

Len Ennever   Project Director

Albert James   Deputy Project Director

Wynne Harlen   Evaluator

Sheila Parker
Don Radford
Mary Horn

Made and printed by Waterlow (Dunstable) Limited

General preface

'Science 5/13' is a project sponsored jointly by the Schools Council, the Nuffield Foundation and the Scottish Education Department and based at the University of Bristol School of Education. It aims at helping teachers to help children between the ages of five and thirteen years to learn science through first-hand experience using a variety of methods.

The Project produces books that comprise Units dealing with subject areas in which children are likely to conduct investigations. Some of these Units are supported by books of background information. The Units are linked by objectives that the Project team hopes children will attain through their work. The aims of the Project are explained in a general guide for teachers called *With objectives in mind* which contains the Project's guide to Objectives for children learning science, reprinted at the back of each Unit.

Acknowledgements

The Project is deeply grateful to its many friends: to the local education authorities who have helped us work in their areas, to those of their staff, who acting as area representatives, have borne the heavy brunt of administrating our trials and to the teachers, heads and wardens who have been generous without stint in working with their children on our materials. The books we have written drew substance from the work they did for us, and it was through their critical appraisal that our materials reached their present form. For guidance we had our sponsors, our Consultative Committee and, for support in all our working, the University of Bristol. To all of them we acknowledge our many debts: their help has been invaluable.

Metrication

This has given us a great deal to think about. We have been given much good advice by well-informed friends, and we have consulted many reports by learned bodies. Following the advice and the reports wherever possible we have expressed quantities in metric units with Imperial units afterwards in square brackets if it seemed useful to state them so.

There are, however, some cases to which the recommendations are difficult to apply. For instance we have difficulty with units such as miles per hour (which has statutory force in this country) and with some Imperial units that are still in current use for common commodities and, as far as we know, liable to remain so for some time. In these cases we have tried to use our common sense, and in order to make statements that are both accurate and helpful to teachers we have quoted Imperial measures followed by the approximate metric equivalent in square brackets if it seemed sensible to give them.

Where we have quoted statements made by children, or given illustrations that are children's work, we have left unaltered the units in which the children worked—in any case some of these units were arbitrary.

Contents

Introduction

Science with young children is primarily concerned with gathering experience. Infants have a natural curiosity about their surroundings and almost any work or play that concerns exploration of their environment results in learning with understanding. In contrast the following story told by a teacher about a conversation she had with her six-year-old niece underlines the results of teaching divorced from experience.

Child	I get all my mental sums wrong.
Aunt	What does your teacher say ?
Child	A man sold a horse for £5 and made £3 profit. What's profit, auntie ?
Aunt	What did the teacher say next ?
Child	What did he buy it for ? I put 'for riding'.
Aunt	What did the teacher say to that ?
Child	She marked it with a cross. I decided it was wrong because a man would not sell a horse if he liked riding.
Aunt	If the man had paid £2 for the horse and sold it for £5, what would this tell you ?
Child	He got £3 for buying and selling it.
Aunt	Well, that's his profit.
Child	Oh, well I can do them all now. They are all like that.
Aunt	Now be careful, the teacher might say 'what did he gain ?' This would have the same meaning as profit.
Child	Is it just like gaining a pound on the bathroom scales ?
Aunt	Yes.
Child	Is that profit ?
Aunt	No, it is profit only when it is money.

'Probably', as the aunt said, 'the next time my niece hears the word *prophet* it will be from somewhere in the Old Testament.'

Most teachers will agree that it is better for children to look at real things that are part of their world and to find out about these things for themselves. They do so, with help and guidance from the teacher, by methods that are in essence scientific. Most of the knowledge a young child gains is obtained by a process of trial and error. He finds, when playing with water, that it will not run uphill ; when planting seeds in the garden that those he puts too deep never appear as seedlings. He is continually comparing one thing with another and gains from his comparisons and his sorting a pattern of understanding.

These methods used unconsciously by children are the methods that a scientist uses consciously in his process of 'finding out', they are really just extensions of the abilities present in every individual which enable him to find out about his world. They are the latent forces which Nathan Isaacs speaks of as making children of five entering school ready to 'enjoy exploring, manipulating, experimenting, comparing, trying to discover causes and think up the right explanations, discussing and arguing and putting to the test'.

Elspeth Huxley has given a description of a modern infant classroom that it would be hard to better :

'Providing things for small children to discover is the prime function of the nursery and infant school. A rich environment this is called. Rich it is indeed ; a fantastic conglomeration of paints and brushes, Plasticine and clay, old stockings, jars and tins ; cartons that have once held cereals,

1

detergents, cigarettes, sugar, almost anything under the sun ; hammers and nails, scissors and paste, berries and nuts, teasels and twigs, shells and old birds' nests, spiders in jars, live guinea pigs, wooden spoons—it would be totally impossible to list a tenth of all objects to be seen. The teacher must have eyes not merely in the back of her head, but all over like spangles on a pearly queen. She must always be on hand, but never obtrusive, a sort of universal presence, like God, only more interfering ; she does at least stop children battering each other on the head if necessary—if she does her job well it scarcely ever is. Small children doing something active seldom quarrel, it is boredom that makes bullies, every nursery teacher knows this and most mothers but as yet few politicians.'

It is hoped that the suggestions set out in this text will fit naturally into such a context. *They are simply possible things to do and not a scheme of work to be carried out.* Many an infant teacher has been heard to say 'I don't do any science'. Look at what is suggested, you may be surprised at how much you already do.

Investigations invite questions, those asked by the children are usually the best ones to pursue, but this does not preclude those from the teacher. Many questions are asked in this Unit. They spring from knowledge of the types of question children ask and are taken from areas in which they tend to show most interest. A teacher's individual experience will be a good guide in judging their relevance to his or her situation.

Fairly spontaneous investigation, both indoors and out, will lead to all sorts of activity. Counting, measuring, ordering, symmetry, timing, estimating, making charts, painting, writing, modelling will all come about naturally. Much of this discovery work stimulates good creative writing by which vocabulary is greatly enlarged. Pleasing poems can be written when there is something to write about or something that has stimulated the imagination. Sometimes these poems can be turned into a song. Stories have been made up to fit the work on shadow puppets and sounds have

been used as 'noises off' in drama work. A great impetus is given to reading, painting and modelling and often dancing is tied up with the work on shadows.

Science is but a part of the wide world of a young child. Yet the methods of science are his natural way of exploring it. He will use them with or without our help but he will use them to far greater advantage if we recognise them too and encourage him. This text is a humble attempt to help in this sensitive, often difficult but rewarding task.

Infants and objectives

Strongly underpinning the work of this Project is the idea of objectives. * Objectives are statements of what we are aiming to bring about through the activities and experiences we make available to children. You will see that the objectives the Project team thinks it desirable for infants to attain are more general than those in the rest of the list. Science in the infant classroom is very much interwoven into the activities that normally go on there, it is indistinguishable as a separate activity and the objectives relate to much more than what could be called 'scientific ideas'.

Developing attitudes, interests and aesthetic awareness
Willingness to ask questions.
Willingness to handle both living and non-living material.
Sensitivity to the need for giving proper care to living things.
Enjoyment in using all the senses for exploring and discriminating.
Willingness to collect material for observation or investigation.

*See With objectives in mind

2

Encouragement of observing, exploring and ordering observations
Appreciation of the variety of living things and materials in the environment.
Awareness of changes which take place as time passes.
Recognition of common shapes—square, circle, triangle.
Recognition of regularity in patterns.
Ability to group things consistently according to chosen or given criteria.

Developing basic concepts and logical thinking
Awareness of the meaning of words which describe various types of quantity.
Appreciation that things which are different may have features in common.

Posing questions and devising experiments or investigations to answer them
Ability to find answers to simple problems by investigation.
Ability to make comparisons in terms of one property or variable.

Acquiring knowledge and learning skills
Ability to discriminate between different materials.
Awareness of the characteristics of living things.
Awareness of properties which materials can have.
Ability to use displayed reference material for identifying living and non-living things.

Communicating
Ability to use new words appropriately.
Ability to record events in their sequences.
Ability to discuss and record impressions of living and non-living things in the environment.
Ability to use representational symbols for recording information on charts or block graphs.

Appreciating patterns and relationships
Awareness of cause/effect relationships.

Interpreting findings critically
Awareness that the apparent size, shape and relationships of things depend on the position of the observer.

If children achieve such objectives we may be sure that they will have pursued work that has a strong scientific flavour. It is useful to bear either these objectives, or preferably your own objectives, in mind when carrying out activities such as those suggested in the text and to return, now and again, to look at them and consider how well they are being achieved.

Our thesis is this : we have tried to point out to infant teachers the science that lies embedded in the work they already do ; our hope is that they will see links between their classroom activities that they have not seen before and be able to make them of deeper significance both to the children and to themselves. Lastly we hope that they will see their work in better relation to a continued education for children, planned at least as far as its science content is concerned.

Sunny day things

The following activities involve children in exploring space, time and movement.

Following the sun

Look at the position of the sun at different times of the day.

Following the sun across the window

12 noon

9 am   3 pm

The beginning and end of the school day and noon are particularly suitable. (Warn the children not to look directly at the sun.) From such an activity children might develop an appreciation of time within the day.

Gradually an awareness of where the sun rises and where it sets might develop.

What do a sunrise and a sunset look like, and what changes in colour occur? What sorts of

Following a shadow

paintings can children make to record these events?

Record the position of the sun by fixing tape to the window as the sun traverses the sky.

Or fix a marker to the window and follow the shadow cast down the wall.

Shadows

Shadows can be long and thin or short and fat, clear and distinct or faint and fuzzy. In the following activities children will become more aware of shadows and the change in them due to time of day or position in space of the object casting the shadow. This awareness grows from their own play and there is much in these topics that will bring about discussion, extend vocabulary and entail recording perhaps in drawing or artwork generally, perhaps even in some simple descriptive writing.

What can you do.
I can hop and
shadow?
jump and run and play
But only on a summers
I Cant sing like Boys
day
girls can do But
and
I can nod my head and
curl up too
Russell Wynne

Remember there is often a confusion in an infant's mind between shadows and reflections, which will need to be talked about.

Playing with shadows
Indoors
Inside the classroom it is possible to skirt the sides of a table with curtaining or sheets of sugar paper and let two children play beneath it making shadows using a torch.

Outdoors
What is your shadow like? One six-year-old said, 'It doesn't show my inside—it doesn't show my clothes and buttons'. What is the biggest shadow you can make with your body? The smallest? The longest? The shortest? Does your shadow move when you move? Can you move without your shadow moving? Can you hide your shadow? Can you jump on your shadow?

Try catching shadows on your body, your hand or sheets of paper.

Children can try, in small groups, to make a shadow with four arms, six arms or six legs.

Can you make a shadow with six arms?

Russell Wynne's shadow (see his poem on page 5)

Drawing round shadows

Draw round shadows in the playground using chalk to make a simple outline. How much longer is the shadow than the person who casts it?

One group of infants solved this by drawing round the 'subject' on to sugar paper, cutting out her outline and finding out how many times it went into the length of her shadow.

Try a circus trick—standing on one another's arms (see page 8).

Try casting the shadow on to black sugar paper, drawing round it with chalk and cutting it out.

Can you jump on your shadow?

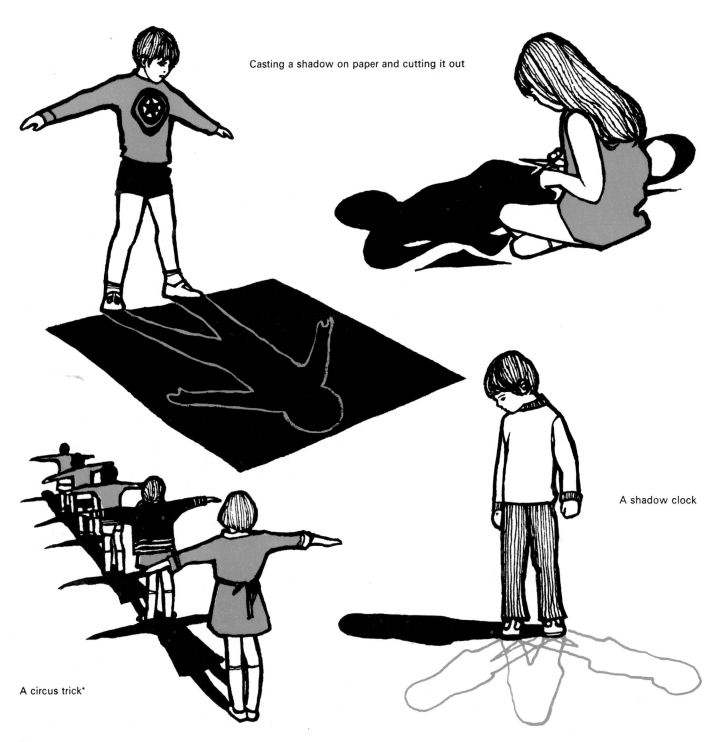

Casting a shadow on paper and cutting it out

A shadow clock

A circus trick*

If a child did this at two different times of the day he would, of course, find that the size of the silhouettes differ. What happens if he draws round his shadow at a number of different times through the day?

In discussion with the teacher he would find that he needs:

A fixed point to work from, which might be got by drawing round his shoes.

To draw in the shadow and record the time. The time might be noted from a clock or, for those children not capable of telling the time, marked in an arbitrary way, for example, at lunch time, at playtime and so on. Alternatively, he could use a plastic bottle instead.

This is quite a difficult activity and seems to be suitable for older, more intelligent infants only.

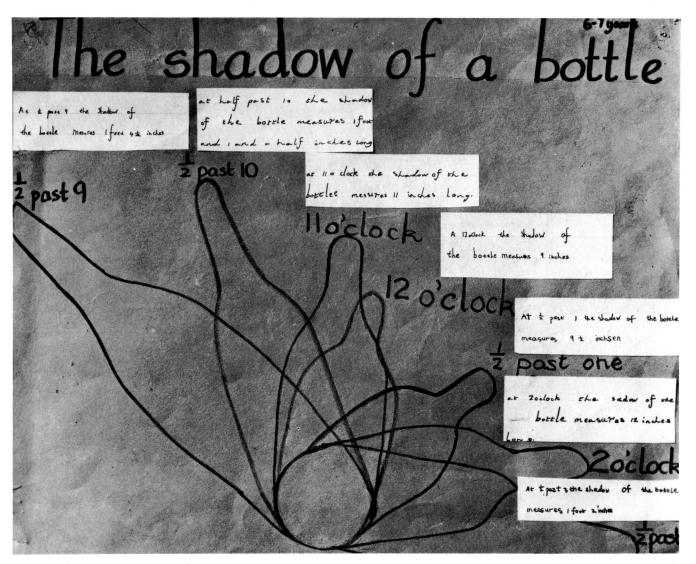

The shadow of a bottle

6-7 years

At ½ past 9 the shadow of the bottle measures 1 foot 4½ inches

at half past 10 the shadow of the bottle measures 1 foot and 1 and a half inches long

at 11 o'clock the shadow of the bottles measures 11 inches long.

A 12 o'clock the shadow of the bottle measures 9 inches

At ½ past 1 the shadow of the bottle measures 9½ inchsen

at 2 o'clock the shadow of the bottle measures 12 inches long.

At ½ past 3 the shadow of the bottle measures 1 foot 2 inches

½ past 9

½ past 10

11 o'clock

12 o'clock

½ past one

2 o'clock

½ past

A human shadow clock

Another shadow clock

It is also interesting to note the position of a shadow at the *same time* each day. Children might mark in the position of their feet with paint and return to the same spot at the same time each day.

Shadow tag

A six-year-old's picture of how he hid his shadow

Making shadows with objects

Take a variety of objects and use them to cast shadows.

What different shadows does an object make?

What shadows do different objects make?

Do these vary with the time of day?

Can you get your shadows to shake hands without touching your own hands together?

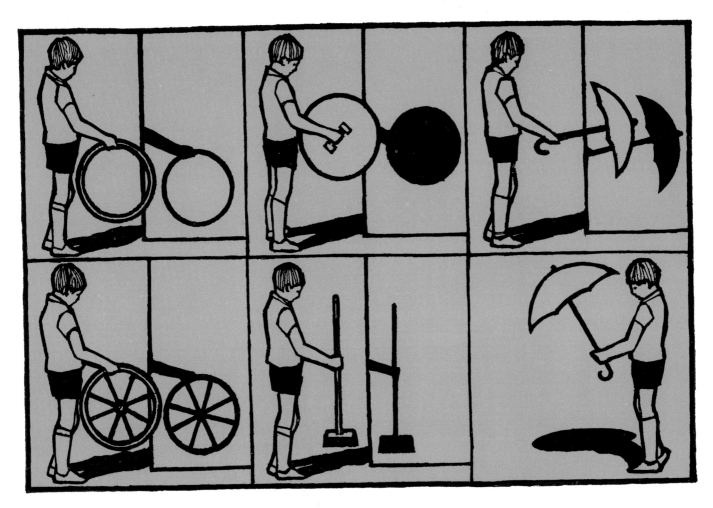

How do these shadows look ? (See the examples given above.)

Can you turn your hoop's shadow into a straight line ?

What is the biggest shadow that can be made with each object ?

What is the smallest ?

One group of six- to seven-year-olds who drew round the shadows cast found that they could get the shadows to fit better on to the paper by moving objects either away from or nearer to the sheets of paper they used.

Shadow games

Shadow games help children examine and develop their awareness of space, teach them much about the properties of shadows and involve them in a great deal of movement and fun.

The following are some suggestions ; children will probably have others of their own.

Stand with your shadow in front of you.
Stand with your shadow behind you.

Touch your shadow. Hide your shadow.

Can you get away from your shadow ?
Can you shake hands with your shadow ?

Chasing shadows

Children can chase one another so that only the shadows touch. Other chasing games might include catching a shadow with your foot, with your hand or with your hand's shadow.

Try enclosing spaces or objects with a shadow.

Some children will lean further and further forward and fall over themselves trying to do this.

Enclosing a stone with a shadow

Catch

A group of six children stand in a circle with a seventh child (the chaser) at the centre. The six children make up two teams of three which can be given names. The chaser shouts out the name of one of the teams and that team runs as quickly as it can, with *hands linked*, to a 'home' base whilst pursued by the shadow of the chaser. Should the chaser's shadow touch that of one of the three children running away then that child becomes the chaser.

Stamping on shadows

In this game a circle of about 5 m, say, in diameter is drawn on the playground. A limited number of children run about in the circle with one 'chaser'. When the chaser steps on a shadow, he calls out 'stop' and that child stands on the spot until the game ends. The last child caught becomes the 'chaser' in the next game.

Shadow plays

Children can improvise and perform shadow plays using cut-out figures and solid objects to cast the shadows.

These might be performed on a wall outdoors using sunlight. Indoors shadows can be thrown on a wall or the blackboard. A screen also shows up shadows especially if you use a table lamp with a 100 W clear bulb or a slide projector as the light source.

One class of six- and seven-year-olds improvised the following shadows using their hands and bodies : a butterfly, a witch, a chimney, a snake, a man with a spear, a gangster with two guns, a crocodile, a bird and a bat.

| Hand shadows: a llama | Cut-out figures on sticks | Solid objects on a table |

Looking up

In exploring the outdoor world there is a tendency to forget the world above us. Lie on the grass or on groundsheets and look at it more intently. Be careful not to look directly at the sun.

Cirrus cloud formation

What can be seen?

Children will probably say the sun and clouds, perhaps an aeroplane, perhaps birds, perhaps a smoke trail left by a jet, perhaps tops of trees. How would they describe what they see? Draw some pictures.

Children drawing clouds, for example, will begin

Cumulus cloud formation

to realise that these have a definite shape. If they are interested enough to look over a period of changing weather conditions they will become aware that there are differently shaped clouds. Eventually children may recognise some of the main cloud types by shape if not by name:

cumulus clouds—cauliflower shaped

cirrus clouds—high, thin wispy

nimbus clouds—dark and threatening.

If you change your position does anything in the sky change?

What is moving?

Which things in the sky are moving? Are some things moving faster than others? Are some things moving at the same rate? Children will probably say the clouds are moving at the same rate—how do they know this? Are all the things above the children at the same height?

Moon and stars

The moon and stars sometimes show in late afternoon. What shape is the moon? Try noting its shape through successive evenings in winter, when it rises before children's bedtime, and make a classroom chart to illustrate its phases. Such work often brings about a gradual awareness of where the moon rises.

Do you get shadows during moonlight?

Recording

Looking at the sky might result in children painting pictures showing clouds or perhaps the sun in differing positions. It might result in imaginative work. Many people see a face in the moon or an old man carrying a bundle of sticks. What do the children see? Can they show what they see in their paintings?

Discuss what things look like, which things in the sky are *bigger* than others, which are moving *faster* than others and which things are *higher* than others.

The wind

Which direction does the wind come from?

Let children blow on things, such as a piece of paper or a ping-pong ball. Can they blow a piece of paper towards themselves? They will find that things tend to move away from a wind.

15

Hold up a wet finger. The side that dries most quickly will feel colder. This is the side the wind is coming from.

Pluck a handful of grass and let it fall. Hold up a hanky.

Look at smoke from a chimney.

Make a windsock

All these things will help to tell wind direction.

What does the wind do?
Look for things that the wind does.

It blows things along : paper in the gutter, washing on the line, sailing boats, kites.

It holds things up : gliders, parachutes, birds.

All these aspects make a good basis for a large collage. Drying rates of washing are discussed in the chapter 'Rainy day things'. Sailing boats, gliders and parachutes are all considered in the chapter 'Doing things'.

One group of six-year-olds investigated the strength of the wind by seeing how far it would blow a long piece of card hung from a string.

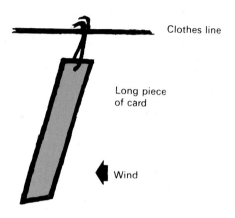

A card wind indicator

This led them to trying pieces of card of varying width.

Which of these will be blown highest by the wind ?

Doing things

Infants enjoy doing things. Theirs is a world of make-believe where a shoebox may become a 'cot' and an inverted table a 'boat'. Blocks, boxes, planks, tins, wood, canes, cardboard tubes, constructional apparatus—an endless variety of materials are used ; in fact children are only limited in their play by the variety and quantity available, their imagination does the rest. Science is incidental in such play—it very much takes a back seat—the activity itself, the freedom of expression and the sheer delight in having made something are what are important.

Where is this science?

Firstly, embedded in the activities themselves are things that are basically scientific. Children building an Indian totem pole from boxes, for example, must consider the size of the boxes and which surfaces will fit best for stability. Even a simple wall built from blocks must be vertical for stability, and certain arrangements of blocks are more stable than others.

Which wall is easiest to knock over ?

Who can make the tallest tower of bricks ?

Secondly, science is the handmaiden that helps in an activity. For example, having made a model lighthouse it is fun to set a light flashing from it.

Lighting things

Make a simple electric circuit.

All you need are a torch bulb (3·5 V), a bulb-holder, a battery (4·5 V) and some single-strand bell wire.

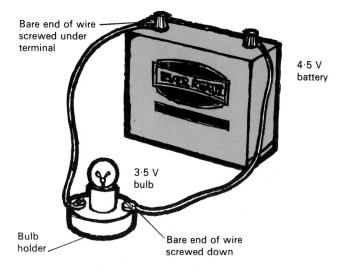

Bare end of wire screwed under terminal

4·5 V battery

3·5 V bulb

Bulb holder

Bare end of wire screwed down

Many young children have difficulty manipulating screws, wire and screwdrivers. They will need to be helped.

Single-strand bell wire is covered by a plastic sheath. This must be removed at the ends and the wire used to make a connection.

The wire should be looped under the screw so that the wire is pulled under the screw as it is tightened.

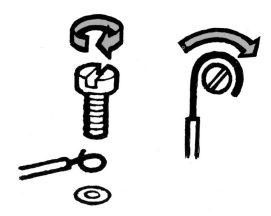

The real purpose of such a circuit is to do a 'job of work'. Some suggestions follow.

Wiring a shoebox doll's house

Attach the bulb to the lid, and invert the lid to form the roof of the house.

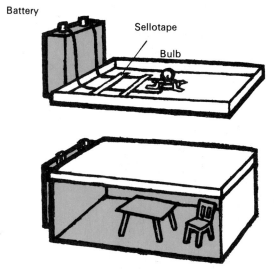

Battery

Sellotape

Bulb

The bulb stays on permanently unless there is a loose connection in the wiring. That is, if there is a gap where the wire joins the bulb-holder or where it joins the terminals of the battery. The bulb will also fail to light if it is loose in its socket.

There are two scientific ideas embedded in such experience :

A continuous metal circuit is necessary for the bulb to light.

A gap in the circuit is equivalent to a switch.

In the shoebox room the mere act of uncoupling one of the wires from the battery is a sufficient 'switch'. The same sort of circuit might be used to light other models.

Eyes on a robot

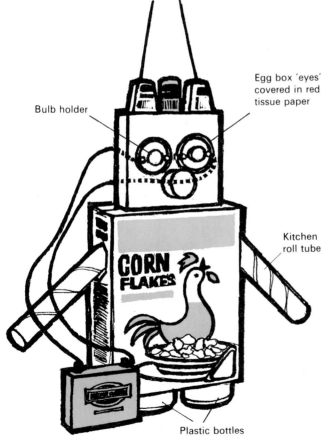

Bulb holder

Egg box 'eyes' covered in red tissue paper

Kitchen roll tube

Plastic bottles

CORN FLAKES

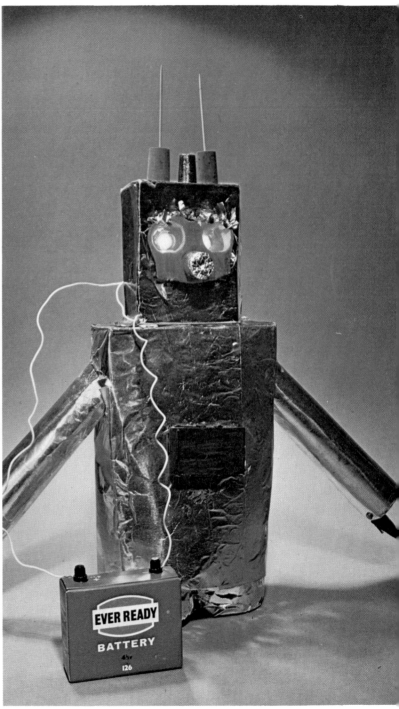

EVER READY BATTERY

Headlights on a car

What difference does wiring in these alternative ways make?

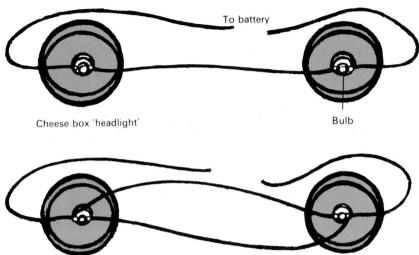

Cheese box 'headlight'　　　　　　　　　　Bulb

To battery

A lighthouse

A lighthouse is easily made by fixing your circuit through a salt carton and meat-paste jar.

It is easy to make the light flash by having one loose wire which is repeatedly tapped against the terminal of the battery.

The terminal cap has been removed.

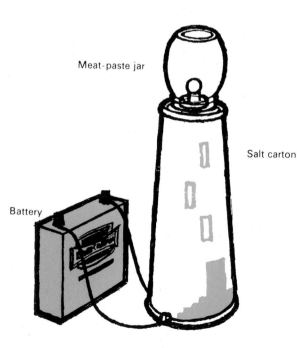

Meat-paste jar

Salt carton

Battery

Put in a switch. It will have to be very simply made for children to understand it.

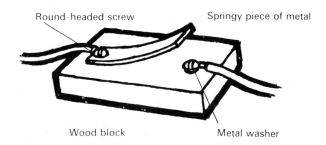

Round-headed screw · Springy piece of metal

Wood block · Metal washer

Here is one idea.

Repeated tapping of the switch will cause the bulb to flash.

Some children will probably find by accident (especially if suitable materials are left to hand) that the gap left in the circuit when the switch is open can be bridged by materials that will cause the bulb to light.

What things will do this? *Conductors*

What things will not do this? *Insulators*

Put pieces of metal, spoons, forks, a ruler, a plastic beaker, coins, keys, tin lids and so on, out for the children to try.

A bell on the Wendy house
We can use electricity to do other things as well as light bulbs.

Why not put a bell at the entrance to the Wendy house?

Can you make a list of all the appliances at home and in school that use electricity?

Things in water

Boats

Use the water trough or an inflatable children's paddling pool for your boats. At its simplest a 'boat' might be just an air-filled bottle, a wood block or a closed tobacco tin.

Which of these moves most easily in the water?

How does the shape affect its method of moving

Boats can be fashioned from card by turning in the edges and Sellotaping them together.

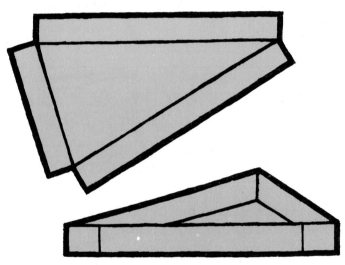

You can also make boats from balsa wood.

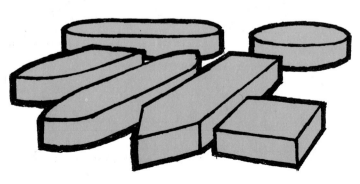

Some schools have made miniboats from corks, pins and coloured paper.

What shaped boats can you make?

What effect does the shape have on the way the boat moves and on its speed?

What ways can you find of making the boat move? Try pushing the water, blowing on the boat, pushing the boat. One group of six-year-olds made their boats move by blowing through drinking straws. As they said 'the air pushes the water and the water pushes the boat'—a real experience of transfer of energy.

Fit some sails made from paper, card or Perspex. What shapes can the children think of?

Wooden meat skewer

Children often make the sails too tall and the boats overbalance—they realise distribution of weight is important. Look at a toy yacht and decide what helps its stability.

Try blowing the boats across the pool. Doing this with an electric fan with plastic blades is fun.

Which shapes of sail are best? Try the sails in different positions. Which shapes of sail are best when blown by the fan?

Disturb the water at the edge of a pool and compare movement of the boats in still water with movement in choppy water. Have a race.

A powered boat is easily made from balsa wood.

Which way must you wind the paddle to make the boat travel forward?

Things in the air

Gliders

Begin by dropping things. A flat piece of paper, a large ball, a small ball, a squeezy bottle, a feather, a balloon, a cotton reel and so on. Which will fall straight down? Which float down?

Fill a balloon with air and another with water. Which comes down first?

Make some gliders. Fold a sheet of paper as shown.

This is probably the simplest form of glider that children can make.

What holds it up?

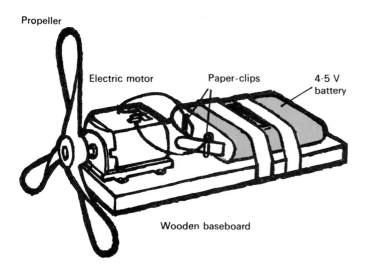

An electric fan

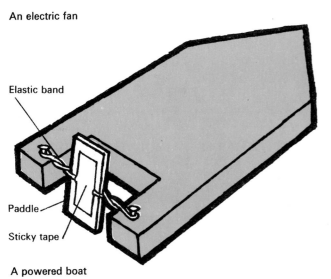

A powered boat

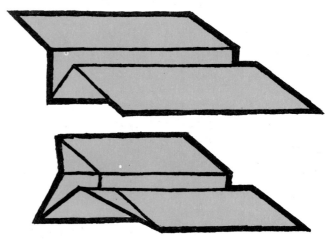

Here is another way to make a glider. Fold the paper as shown and cut out the shaded areas with scissors.

Boys often buy plastic and balsa-wood gliders. How well do these travel in the air? Whose can go furthest?

Try flying them indoors and outdoors. Make gliders from card, paper, balsa and other woods and polystyrene. Which flies best? Which goes furthest? Make a graph.

Try a circular glider—a paper plate is ideal.

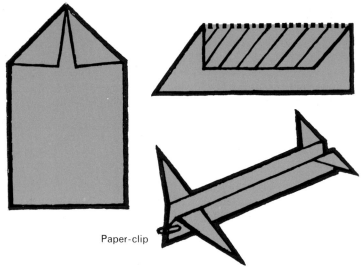

Paper-clip

Parachutes
Make some parachutes, screw them up and throw them in the air.

Are some materials better than others for making parachutes?

Compare a sheet of cotton with one of plastic or wool.

Why does the parachute come down slowly?

What does a parachute without a hole at its centre do?

Does the size of the hole have any effect on the descent of the parachute?

Shuttlecock
Throw it in the air.

Why does it float down?

What happens if you weight the cork with Plasticine?

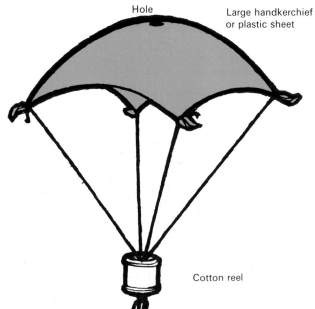

Hole

Large handkerchief or plastic sheet

Cotton reel

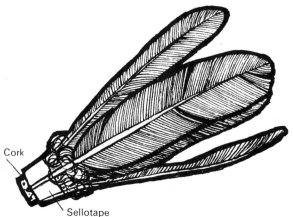

Cork

Sellotape

Kites

Start by blowing pieces of paper along.
Have a race.

Try it across a hall or down a corridor from a fixed starting point. Is it fair for everyone to have the same size piece of paper? Does the size matter anyway?

Make some paper fans and blow your pieces of paper along with the fans. Who wins this race?

How far can you blow a piece of paper with *one* blow? Measure the distance. How far can your best friend blow it?

Now try getting a polystyrene ceiling tile up in the air by making a kite. There will need to be some adult help here.

Take your ceiling tile and mark its centre.
Make another spot 12 cm above it as shown.

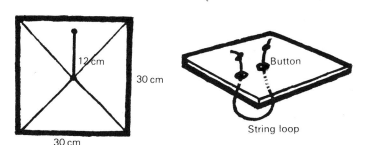

12 cm

30 cm

30 cm

Button

String loop

If you run along the playground with your kite it should take off but you will need a windy day for it to fly well.

What can you find that your kite will lift?
Will it pull a toy lorry or a roller-skate along?

Make a hole through both these marks with a knitting needle.

Thread some string through and tie it to two buttons.

Fix a towing line and stick some paper streamers about 3 m long at the base of the tile.

Make sure the towing line is fixed near the centre of the string loop. It may need adjusting to get the kite working properly.

Streamers

Towing line

25

Windmills

Again a task requiring some dexterity. Many children will need help.

Take a large square of paper.

Cut it as shown.

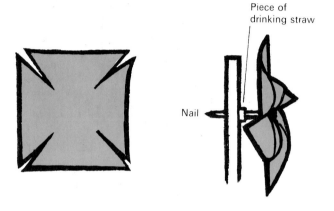

Piece of drinking straw

Nail

Turn in alternate corners to the centre in turn. Pin the corners in place with a nail, which is then driven into a stick. Put a bead or a piece of drinking straw between the paper and the stick to reduce the friction.

Try fixing a windmill to a balsa wood glider.

How does it perform when dropped from an upstairs window?

Can you find some sycamore fruits to drop as well?

Things on land

A tin lid roller

Put some marbles under a tin lid with a straight-sided edge (a coffee jar lid is suitable) and you have a structure which moves.

Who can make it go furthest across the hall?

How far is this distance?

If you vary the number of marbles does it make any difference to the way the lid moves? The speed at which it moves?

What happens if you put a brick on the tin lid?

How could you move a brick? Try pencils, marbles or a trolley.

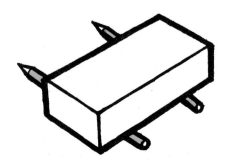

A tin-can roller

Punch two holes in both the lid and the bottom of a tin can. Thread strong elastic through as shown and hang a weight at the centre.

Roll the can forward. Why does it return?

Who can get it to make the longest return journey?

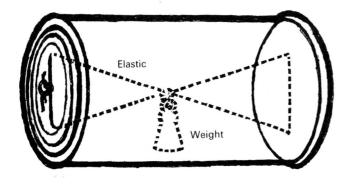

A 'tank'

What effect does number of turns of the match-stick have on distance travelled?

What effect does number of turns of the match-stick have on how fast the tank goes?

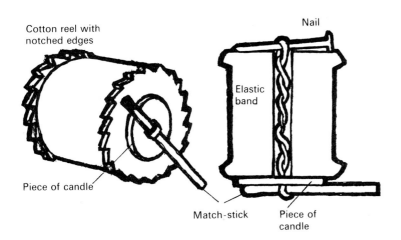

Cotton reel with notched edges

Nail

Elastic band

Piece of candle

Match-stick

Piece of candle

How long does a tank take to move down a fixed stretch of corridor? Whose tank wins a race?

Balancing toys

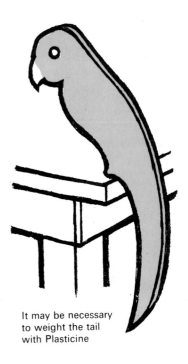

Parrot cut from thick card

It may be necessary to weight the tail with Plasticine

A perching parrot

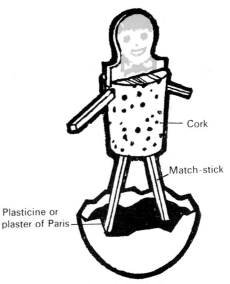

Cork

Match-stick

Plasticine or plaster of Paris

Egg-shell or half a ping-pong ball

A wobbly man

Cranes

A number of children have visited the docks or building sites and made cranes. Here are two suggestions from schools.

A large crane

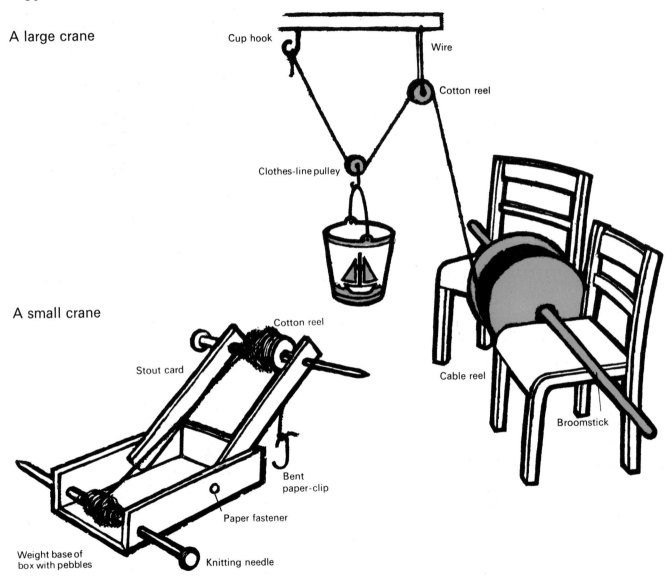

Cup hook

Wire

Cotton reel

Clothes-line pulley

A small crane

Cotton reel

Stout card

Bent paper-clip

Cable reel

Broomstick

Paper fastener

Weight base of box with pebbles

Knitting needle

Pattern and symmetry

A favourite activity with children is making things by cutting and folding pieces of paper.

Make a rosette.

Fold pleats into a piece of paper.

Bind it at the centre with thread.

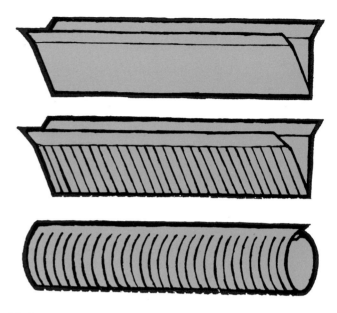

Fan the ends out and paste together to make a circle.

Make a flower.

Fold a piece of paper and crease it about 1 cm from the top.

Make parallel cuts as far as this crease, then overlap the uncut edges and paste them together.

The two ends can then be pasted together.

Use thread to suspend the flower.

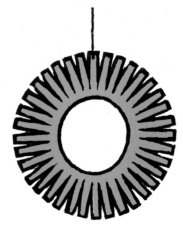

Cut some patterns in folded paper. These are often symmetrical, as are many objects in an infant's world. Some of the drawings children make show they have an innate ability to produce pictures with some sort of balance or symmetry—this is clearly seen in almost any infant's drawing of a face.

Look at shapes and patterns in the environment. What sorts of shapes are there in the classroom, in doors, windows, wallpaper, clothes, floor, walls and ceiling? Outdoor possibilities are limitless for there are patterns in most natural objects, in a flower, a leaf or a woodlouse, whilst symmetry in man-made objects such as walls, railings and buses is also worth discussing.

Notice how the pattern may *radiate out about a point* as when one looks down on the cut half of an orange or on a sea-urchin shell, how it may be a *repeating pattern* as in a caterpillar, a string of beads, a bamboo pole or a wooden fence or how *one half may mirror* the other as in a butterfly or indeed a child itself.

One class investigated the patterns in different car tyres and made rubbings and plaster casts of them. Try making patterns showing radial, repeating and bilateral symmetry with peas, beans, sweet corn, rice, split peas, tiny coloured beads or stones, buttons, curtain hooks, pieces of paper, lino tiles, Plasticine and so on.

Collect as many examples as you can. Wallpapers are a good source.

What sort of pattern or symmetry do you have in the maypole?

Listening to things

Listening to sounds

Indoors
What sounds are there in a normal busy classroom ? Voices, children moving about, chairs scraping, pencils moving on paper, water slurping. Children will find many more.

What sounds are there if everyone is still ? Breathing, heartbeats, a clock ticking, coughing.

in the class Jonathan room children I can hear there friends talking to Walking on the and people and People the floor chairs about Pushing Voices and and Watches other ing and the tick breathing

Outdoors
What sounds are there outdoors ? Go on a 'listening walk'. There will be noises from traffic, birds and other animals, the wind, footsteps and so on. Write down the sounds you hear.

Back in the classroom the sounds can be discussed. Words can be sought to fit them. The *chirp* of a bird, the *thump* of a heartbeat, the *crunch* of footsteps on gravel.

Sorting the sounds
Which sounds are loud, which soft ? Which sounds are pleasant, which unpleasant ? Were there any sounds warning of danger ? What other ways can you think of to sort sounds ?

What sounds do the children like to hear ?

A man playing the piano.

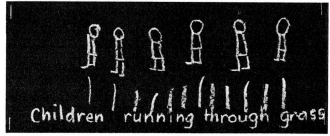

Children running through grass

Making sounds

Make sounds in the classroom. Almost any object will make a sound if shaken, tapped or

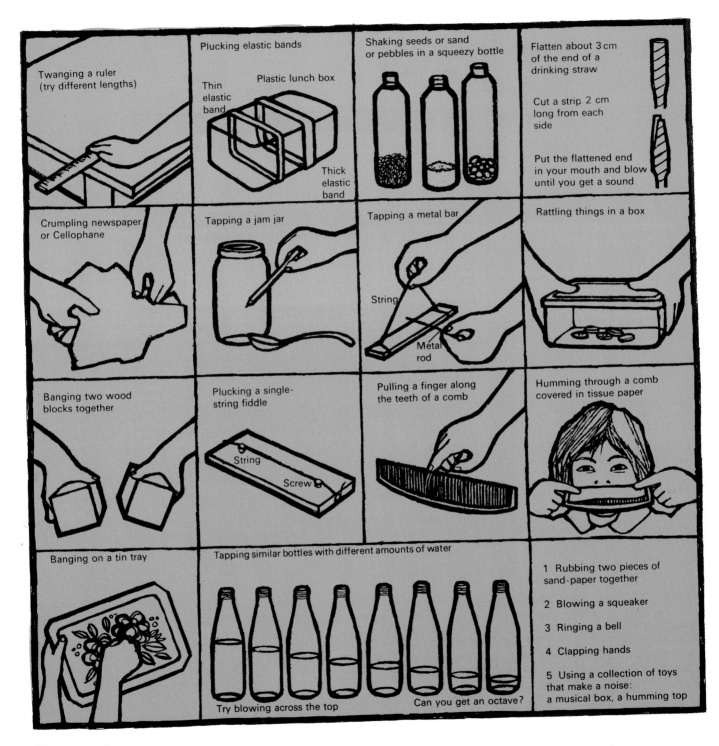

Twanging a ruler (try different lengths)

Plucking elastic bands

Thin elastic band

Plastic lunch box

Thick elastic band

Shaking seeds or sand or pebbles in a squeezy bottle

Flatten about 3 cm of the end of a drinking straw

Cut a strip 2 cm long from each side

Put the flattened end in your mouth and blow until you get a sound

Crumpling newspaper or Cellophane

Tapping a jam jar

Tapping a metal bar

String

Metal rod

Rattling things in a box

Banging two wood blocks together

Plucking a single-string fiddle

String

Screw

Pulling a finger along the teeth of a comb

Humming through a comb covered in tissue paper

Banging on a tin tray

Tapping similar bottles with different amounts of water

Try blowing across the top

Can you get an octave?

1 Rubbing two pieces of sand-paper together

2 Blowing a squeaker

3 Ringing a bell

4 Clapping hands

5 Using a collection of toys that make a noise: a musical box, a humming top

crumpled. Make a class collection of objects that make sounds. Some children might like to make a pictorial chart of all the ways they have found of making noises. There are some suggested ways of making sounds shown on the opposite page.

Make up games. Tap a desk, a chair, a jam jar, a radiator, a window pane and so on. Then listen with eyes shut whilst someone taps these things all over again. Can you follow the sequence?

Children can improvise ways of making sounds for noises off-stage in drama work or sound effects when telling a story. What sounds do classroom pets make?

What makes the sound?

In all cases associated with the sounds children hear there is some sort of vibration involved. In musical instruments it might be the strings, the skin on a drum or the column of air inside an organ pipe.

It is difficult for many young children to grasp that vibrations are usually associated with sounds, but most of them will appreciate that there has been some form of movement in the 'apparatus' with which they have been playing. Wherever possible, attention can be drawn to this; vibrating elastic bands and a twanging ruler are good examples.

Look for vibrations wherever you make a sound. A hand gently placed on a vibrating voice box, on the wooden case of a guitar as the strings are plucked, on the piano case when the keys are struck or holding cymbals after they have clashed together all emphasise this point.

The vibrations of the skin of a drum show clearly if seeds are placed on it and it is then struck.

Try making your own drum.

Glue a piece of Terylene firmly to the top of a large empty tin. Wet the cloth and let it dry. Then starch it, let it dry again and paint the Terylene with aeroplane dope.

High and low sounds

How can high sounds be made? Try plucking a tightly drawn elastic band, tapping the short keys on a xylophone, twanging a short length of a ruler projecting from a table, singing, plucking the thin strings on a guitar.

How can low sounds be made? Try banging two wood blocks together, plucking the thick string on a guitar, twanging a long length of a ruler projecting from a table, singing, stamping on the floor.

Tap a range of objects hung on strings.

What notes do you get?

Can you play a tune?

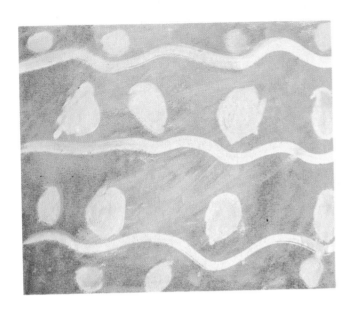

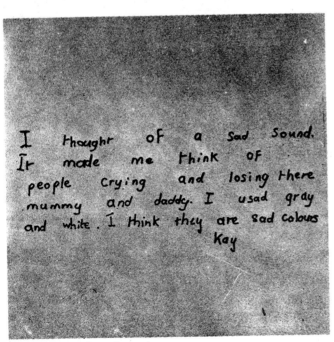

I thought of a sad sound. It made me think of people crying and losing there mummy and daddy. I usad gray and white. I think they are sad colours
                                    Kay

Kay's painting of a sad sound

Happy Sounds
I thought of a Happy Sound, It made me think of colours and people playing. I thought of a party and jelly and blamonje. I made a happy pattern
                                    Tracy

Tracy's painting of a happy sound

Different-sized nails can also be used to play a tune.

Pluck an elastic band wrapped around a plastic lunch box. What note do you get ? Tighten the band. What note do you get now ? Both thickness and tightness of the elastic band have an effect.

All these experiences can be discussed with children. The following facts might then emerge :

long vibrating lengths—*low notes*

short vibrating lengths—*high notes*

thick vibrating strings give lower notes than thin vibrating strings.

Such findings can be reinforced by examining a variety of instruments. If possible take the front off the piano—look and listen as a long string and then a short string are struck. Examine the strings to see if they vary in thickness. If it is a grand piano many children may suddenly realise why it it is built to a characteristic shape.

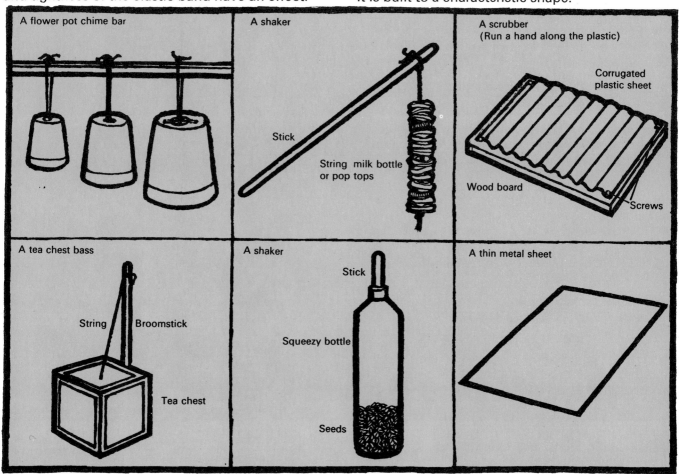

A flower pot chime bar

A shaker

Stick

String milk bottle or pop tops

A scrubber
(Run a hand along the plastic)

Corrugated plastic sheet

Wood board

Screws

A tea chest bass

String   Broomstick

Tea chest

A shaker

Stick

Squeezy bottle

Seeds

A thin metal sheet

Let's have a band

All this work also results in finding that many sounds are melodious. Children might put many of their home-made ways of making sound into forming a band. Much of the apparatus suggested earlier can be used. There are some additional suggestions in the table on the previous page.

Children in one school drew rhythms. Then their teacher played a tune with an obvious 4/4 time pattern. The children were asked to count. When questioned some said, 'I counted 25'; some said, 'I counted 12'; but quite a number said, 'I counted 4 every time.'

The counting was then coupled with clapping and bending on the first beat. This process was repeated with a 3-beats to the bar tune. Children who were asked to identify a tune with a shape on the shapes display quickly placed the 3-beat tune with a triangle, the 4-beat tune with a square and a flowing 6/8 or 5/4 tune with a circle because it rolled on and on.

The counting and drawing of the appropriate shape in the air followed and finally children drew the appropriate shapes on paper. These children were gaining experience of *time* in music.

In making musical instruments, and in using the instruments already present in school, infants will gradually become aware of groups into which their instruments will fit. Some they bang, some they pluck and some they blow. What other classifications can they devise?

Things sound travels through

What does sound travel through? Children will find that sound goes through : the air, solids, liquids. Listen to a pencil tapping a table with ears above and then on the table; a penny tapping a pipe with ears above and then on the pipe; a noise made above and under water in a trough or a swimming bath by banging a piece of metal with a hammer; what is the sound like if you put your ears to the sides of the water trough?

Try banging a wall whilst children, ears pressed against the bricks, stand at the other side; tapping the floor whilst children lie with ears pressed Red Indian fashion to the ground; jangling spoons tied to a string.

Hold the end of the string to your ear.

Jangle the spoons.

What do you hear?

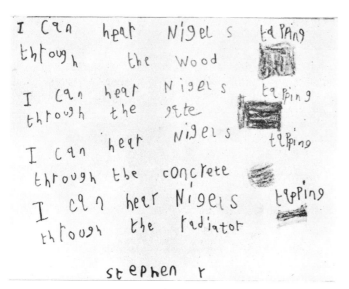

I can hear Nigels tapping through the wood

I can hear Nigels tapping through the gate

I can hear Nigels tapping through the concrete

I can hear Nigels tapping through the radiator

stephen r

Make a yoghurt carton telephone. Does sound travel better through the string or through the air?

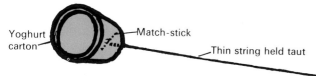

Yoghurt carton — Match-stick — Thin string held taut

Try a telephone made with tins. Are they better than yoghurt cartons? Is a thin cocoa tin a better 'tin' telephone than an instant coffee tin?

How far does the sound travel?

If a heating pipe is tapped how far can you go from the classroom and still hear the sound when you press your ear to the pipe? If there are railings around the school how far will sound travel through them?

Measuring can be brought in.

Walk away down a corridor gently tapping a tumbler with a spoon.

How far can you go before your partner cannot hear the sound?

How far can you go before other children cannot hear the sound?

Such distances can be measured in arbitrary or fixed units and plotted on a block graph.

These children would find that they had put themselves in an order of hearing ability.

Some children might point out that tapping a tumbler with a spoon doesn't always give the same volume (amount) of sound. This would be a good point for discussion and from this might arise the need to find something that will give a constant volume of sound. A musical box or a loud ticking clock might do.

A few children may begin to realise that it is difficult to decide at what point they cannot hear a sound moving away from them. Is it better for the sound to come toward you? Why?

Which ear hears best?
A quiet corner is needed for this. Put your chin on the table. Get your partner to slowly bring a ticking watch toward each ear in turn. When do you hear the sound? Can you measure this distance?

Catching sounds

What catches sounds?
Children might suggest ears or the microphone of a hearing aid. Where are ears found?

Draw pictures of one another's ears. Have they all got lobes?

Draw cats' ears and dogs' ears. Collect pictures of animals and discuss where the ears are. This is obvious in many animals, but where are the ears in a frog, an earthworm, a bird, a snake, an insect? Do they have ears?

Such considerations may lead to discussion of the sounds that different animals make:

How do animals make sounds?
What friendly sounds do children's pets make?
What warning sounds do their pets make?
How do birds often signify which is their territory?
Are there any children in the class who speak a second language?

Making sounds louder
How can you make sounds louder? Try cupping your hands around your ears; making a card trumpet to catch the sound

using a toy stethoscope—these are often found in hospital play

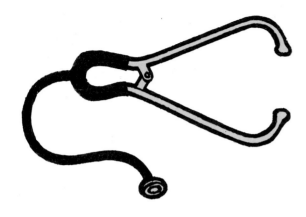

making a stethoscope for one ear

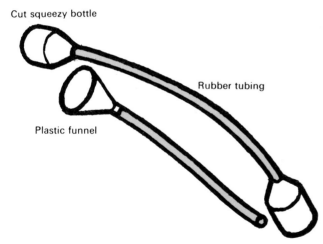

Cut squeezy bottle

Rubber tubing

Plastic funnel

It is important that children do not poke things right into their ears.

Making sounds softer

How can you make sounds softer? Try putting fingers over ears, stuffing cotton wool in ears, or muffling the sound. Muffling sounds can be fun.

One group of children muffled the sound of a transistor radio by lining a shoebox with polystyrene and putting the radio in it.

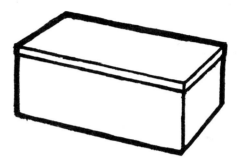

Another group found that a watch could be heard through a jam jar. If they put a duster in the jam jar they found it more difficult to hear the sound from the watch.

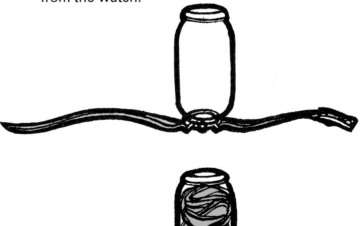

What other ways of muffling sounds can you think of?

Comparing things

Infants enjoy sorting ; buttons, 'conkers', shells, matchboxes, beads are all grist to the mill. They handle, describe and compare objects and gradually develop a vocabulary where words describing size, shape, weight, colour and texture are meaningful.

Sorting objects

Sorting should begin as a permissive individual activity with children placing objects in groups according to criteria they have chosen.

A sorting box is useful.

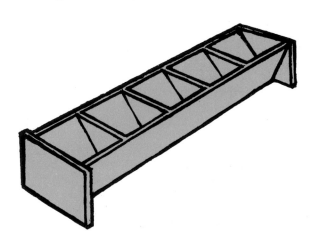

Collecting objects indoors
Collect objects from pockets, desks, cupboards, and sort them. Children usually begin by putting like things together. This is followed by sub-grouping, eg a collection of shells when sorted

from everything else may be sorted on the criterion of shape into cockle shells, limpets, periwinkles, etc. Eventually they progress to sorting based on contrasting qualities such as

shiny and dull
large and small
rough and smooth
soft and hard
heavy and light
warm and cold
bend easily/don't bend easily
dissolve/don't dissolve

All such terms are comparative, not absolute.

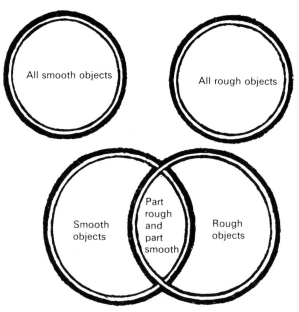

Children like a physical boundary to keep their sorted objects apart.

A hoop or a circle formed from string are suitable.

Objects showing both properties under consideration can be put in a separate group.

One class of six-year-olds compared all the white powders they could find by smelling, weighing the same amount of each, stirring in water and (where safe) by tasting. They did this with lemon pie filling, bicarbonate of soda, baking powder, sponge mix, cream of tartar, granulated sugar, ground rice, Angel Delight, Marvel, Dream Topping, white sauce mix and flour.

Collecting objects outdoors
Children often sort objects collected during a walk. (Perhaps there is even point, at times, in organising a walk to collect objects according to a certain property—see 'Colours' on page 72.)

Which criteria do children choose to sort on: smooth? brown? sticky? shape? size?

Inevitably there are odd items which will need a category of their own—a heading 'undecided objects' may help. Visits to specific places often yield valuable material. A building site, for example, may yield bricks, hardboard, tiles, roofing felt, breeze block, an air brick—all with interesting textures.

Sorting materials

Collect a range of objects made of wood, plastic, metal, wool, cotton, leather, paper, polystyrene, cardboard and glass for children to sort.

Much of an infant's contact with materials comes from handling them in the normal course of classroom activity, eg in making a collage or a model, or during cooking. It is probably as much from these activities as from any conscious sorting that a child comes to distinguish between different materials, to pick out the same material in a variety of objects, and to distinguish between objects made of one material and objects made of more than one material.

Sorting games

It is fun to make up games with an odd man out. For example, one circular object amongst square and rectangular objects, or a 1972 coin amongst a group of 1971 coins.

What sorting games can the children devise to try on their classmates?

Comparing and sorting as they apply to some of the common areas of activity in the classroom

Sand play
Compare sand with other soils by looking, looking with the aid of a magnifying glass, feeling when dry, feeling when damp, feeling when wet.

What things are similar? What things are different? Is the soil dark or light in colour? Is it black, brown, orange or yellow? What new words are there to list?

Children could compare dry and wet sand by making castles, pies, heaps of different heights, shapes and lengths. Questions may arise:

Where does the water go when the sand dries out?

Which can the biggest heap be made from, wet or dry sand?

Measurement of heaps might occur using arbitrary or fixed units.

This is a rough and smooth picture.

The edge is smooth silver paper.

I run my fingers over the fish - the matchsticks feel rough. The paint is smooth. It is a fish picture

This clown is upside down. He is having a rough and tumble

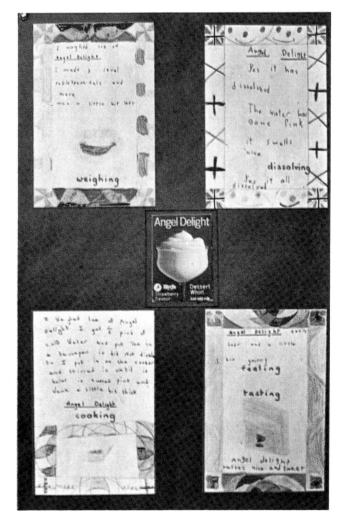

Sorting white powder (see page 41)

The weight of different quantities of sand can be judged by hand or by using a simple balance— terms such as *heaviest, lightest, heavier than, lighter than, the same as,* fit naturally into such a context.

A simple balance might be improvised.

What happens when the same amount of dry sand, eg a yoghurt carton full, is placed on both sides of the balance?

What happens when dissimilar amounts of sand are placed on either side of the balance?

How does the weight of a yoghurt carton full of damp sand compare with that of a yoghurt carton full of dry sand?

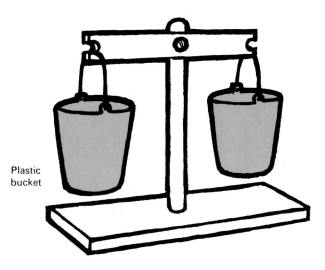

Plastic bucket

Children might compare drying rates of sand by the following method. How long do the *same amounts* of damp and very wet sand take to dry? What changes occur as sand dries?

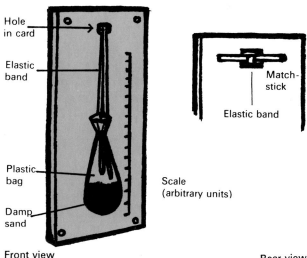

Hole in card

Elastic band

Plastic bag

Damp sand

Front view

Match-stick

Elastic band

Scale (arbitrary units)

Rear view

Water play
How much
Children pouring water from one container to another note the different shapes the water takes and the change in height.

What is the same amount of water like in different containers?

Many children think that the *amount* of water increases or decreases as the water moves from container to container. (These need a lot of experience of water play.) It is as well to question what they mean by amount—is the child answering wrongly or just answering a different question?

How many times will one container contribute to the filling of another container? For example, *about* twenty milk bottles full of water might be needed to fill a large tin, and *about* three to fill the squeezy bottle. The approximate nature of measuring is becoming clearer.

A range of bottles and jars can be compared. Which holds most? Which holds least? Which hold the same?

How long
A tin or a squeezy bottle with a hole in its base forms a simple measuring device.

Compare a bottle with a large hole with one with a small hole.

Make a small hole by covering the nozzle of a squeezy bottle with Plasticine and pushing a pin through.

Children will be getting experience of the *duration of events* and comparing one event with another. Vocabulary involves terms such as longer than, shorter than, as long as.

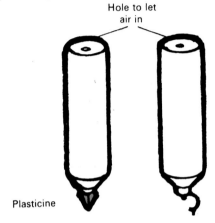

A digression on timing
Very young children of about five years often have difficulty with a *sequence of events.* Try presenting some of them with pictures showing events that happen during the day. Can they put the pictures in order? Many will find this difficult. Making a picture clock of the school-day with pictures mounted to illustrate various events; lunch time and so on, may help the children.

Compare things that move quickly with those that move slowly, and cut pictures that fit each category from magazines and mount them.

Once children have a good grasp of the sequence of events they can progress to measuring the *duration of events* or to seeing how much they can do in a given time.

How many things can they draw in a minute? The duration of events need not always be timed with a conventional timer, why not time the following events with a water clock?

Skipping.

Hopping the length of the classroom.

Tidying up.

The time taken to fill a large container using a small container.

The time taken to fill the sink with water.

Floating and sinking
Children often compare objects on the criterion of whether they float or sink. Questioning might cause them to take their play a stage further.

How much of an object is above the water surface?

Can children devise ways of sinking floating objects?

Could they sink: a rubber ball, a blown-up balloon, a corked empty bottle, an airtight tin?

Try adding weights or Plasticine or, if appropriate, letting water into the object. In all cases they would be upsetting the weight of the floating object and adding to experience which will become more meaningful at a later age.

Pebbles and rocks
Pebbles
Collect lots of pebbles. Which pebbles are alike? How do pebbles differ in shape, size and colour? What are broken surfaces like?

Sort the pebbles. Make patterns. Put them in groups.

The relative weight of pebbles can be judged by weighing them against arbitrary units. Is a jar of pebbles heavier or lighter than a jar of beans or rice or sand?

Do some pebbles roll more easily than others? Which pebbles will roll most quickly down a slope? What shape helps a pebble roll?

Rocks
Rocks can be compared by the following means:

Looking (Do not forget a magnifier.) What colour are they? What shape?

Touching How hard do they feel? How rough or smooth are they? Do they feel slippery?

Scratching with a coin, a nail file, an iron nail, a paper clip, other rocks.

Cutting with a blunt knife.

Dropping

Polishing with polish and pad.

Grinding with sand-paper, emery paper, or with a mortar and pestle.

Soaking in water

Weighing

Scratching objects with them

Rubbing one rock against another (rubbing sandstone against sandstone gives sand).

What is involved?

Looking
Certain fixed criteria are used in adult schemes of classification so that items can easily be grouped, ordered and identified. Children often sort things without such criteria in mind and a child sorting rocks may, for example, place some in a category such as 'those which I want to keep'. This is a perfectly valid way of sorting; with time and a growing maturity children will come to understand the need for standardisation.

Scratching, cutting, dropping, polishing, grinding
All these methods tell something about the hardness of rocks. They may, however, cause confusion in some children's minds. One rock

may be hard because it does not crumble when pressed, another rock hard because it cannot be easily scratched and yet another rock hard because it does not flake or chip when dropped. All these are methods of comparing the hardness of rocks but *they do not give the same result.* It might be advisable to have a heading or test which just says *scratches* or *crumbles.*

With older infants such work might lead to further refinement; should the *same* implement be used to scratch all rocks? If rocks are dropped would it perhaps be fair to drop them all from the same height? Drop them on to the same surface? The degrees of involvement and the depth of study will naturally depend on the age and stage of development of the child.

Weighing
It is difficult for young children to classify rocks by weight because pieces of rock will differ greatly in size. Most rocks fit into a category which might be termed *medium weight* but it is possible to find a few rocks which children can obviously classify as *light* or *heavy.*

Rocks can be compared against arbitrary weights using a balance and this may give some idea of their relative weight.

Growing things

There is value in having a small number of plants in the classroom. Perhaps cacti and other succulents, a fern, tree seedlings (moss can often be encouraged to grow over the soil at the base of the stem) and some plants bearing flowers such as geraniums. Aquatic plants can grow in the aquarium, perhaps a totally submerged plant such as Canadian pond-weed with a free-floating plant such as duckweed on the water surface. Surrounded by such a variety children soon become conscious of the form and habit of plants.

For the city school with no ground to cultivate, a window box placed against a wall, with trellis-work mounted behind and set out with plants will brighten a dull corner. Bulbs and corms might be planted to provide flowers early in the year; later sweet peas and morning glory could climb the trellis and other flowers such as clarkia occupy the window box. Such an arrangement, apart from its aesthetic value, involves children in planting, tending and carrying out measurements and other simple investigations, not only on the plants but also on the animals, such as insects, which visit the site or will inhabit the soil.

Growing plants in the classroom

Quick growers
Plants are much too static to keep infants interested for long. Begin with quick-growing seeds such as mustard and cress. Plant these out on different media using yoghurt or cream cartons as containers. Damp sand, felt, blotting paper, cloth, cardboard, sawdust, orange peel, a piece of sponge—any media that lie to hand will suffice.

How many seeds were set out in each carton? How many germinate?

The media often dry up. Are there any places in the classroom that are better than others for preventing this happening?

Often children sow such a mass of seeds that it is difficult to see them or to distinguish individual

Sorting seeds

plants once the seeds germinate.

A box with seeds carefully spaced will help the counting.

How many seeds will grow?

What happens if you sow the seeds in pots with different soils? Try sand, a mixture of garden soil and sand, John Innes compost, leaf mould and soil, clay and sand, clay. What happens when seeds are sown far apart?

Quick results also come from the tops of root vegetables. Cut the top off a carrot, turnip or parsnip about 1 cm thick and place it in a saucer with a little water. Leaves soon appear and last quite a long time. Children also like planting cuttings; some are very fast rooting.

Slower growers
Sow some larger seeds. Climbers such as peas and beans and tall plants such as sunflowers create interest. Remember to soak the seeds for about twenty-four hours before sowing. Is there a change in weight after soaking?

It is also worthwhile planting a few seeds in dry soil and noting the effect. What happens to the same seeds given different amounts of water?

What happens:

To seeds that are planted upside down or planted too deeply?

To seedlings grown in a cupboard and thus deprived of light?

If you sow half a seed? Will it give half a plant?

It is worth digging some seeds up a short time after planting. Have they changed in shape or size or in texture? Is anything coming out of the seed? Do frozen peas germinate?

Seeds
Seeds are worth looking at in their own right; they have pleasing shapes and colours, textures and patterns. Make a collection—apple, melon, orange, rice, pomegranate, date, avocado pear, broom, lupin, chestnut, oak, sycamore—there is a fascinating variety.

Children will want to sort and make patterns with them.

Collect fruits and seeds from the actual plants around the school—from a sweet pea pod, from the heart-shaped fruit of the shepherd's purse, from the dandelion clock—children will begin to associate fruits and seeds with flowers.

Look at the hamster food, bird seed and some of the commercial mixtures sold to feed wild birds. What seeds are in these? Sow them. What sort of plants appear?

A bottle garden

Some tree seeds will germinate if planted in wet loam. Chestnut, oak and sycamore do so in the first year but ash takes two years to appear.

A bottle garden
A large sweet jar is ideal but a large jam jar or a Kilner jar will do.

Put a layer of compost in the bottom and let the children put in their plants—ferns, mosses, tradescantia are suitable.

The sides of the jar will sometimes cloud with moisture and all that need be done is to remove the lid for a short time.

Recording
There is no need to make a fetish of recording plant growth. Some plants, such as gourds, grow so fast that their daily increase is *record* enough. It is often the chance remark, the drawing of attention to first shoots or flowers appearing or how a shoot has bent towards the light from the window (what will happen if we turn the pot and leave the plant bending into the classroom?) that is all-important.

A record of increase in height might be made on a marker alongside the plant.

Alternatively, a plant profile might be drawn on a card placed behind the plant.

The profile might be drawn a week later using a different-coloured crayon.

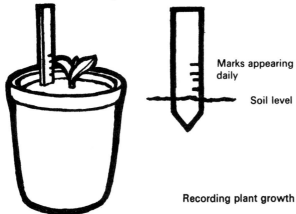

Marks appearing daily

Soil level

Recording plant growth

What changes have occurred?

What sizes are the parts of plants?

A plant profile

Are the leaves the same size all over a plant or do they differ? If they differ where are the biggest leaves?

Do not forget to look at the roots. Shake the soil away from the root of the plant so that its branching nature can be observed. Let the children look at the root hairs (use a magnifier) and talk about how they take in water and 'food' from the soil. How long is the root?

Growing plants outdoors

Tubs and window boxes are useful for growing plants outdoors but ideally each child should have his own small garden. It must be very small, easy to identify and simple to tend. One way of doing this is with a chequer-board garden made up of paving stones and little plots.

Part of each plot might be given over to growing

flowers, bulbs and corms ; nasturtiums, clarkia, sunflowers are all suitable. The annual cycle of seed, plant, flower head, fruit and seed becomes apparent to children. Simple measurements can be made.

How tall is the tallest sunflower?
How many leaves does it have?
How many yellow petals around its edge?
How many fruits does it yield?

Of course the seeds can be kept to sow the following year, some might be used to make patterns or put in a collage, others might be fed to the hamster, for example, sunflower seeds.

Children love to grow things that can be eaten and the rest of the plot might be given over to *crops*—radishes and carrots are especially popular.

How many seeds are planted in each row?
How many plants appear?
Are there more radishes than carrots?

Collect the produce.

What is the total weight of carrots from a plot?
What is the length of the longest carrot?
How much does it weigh?

Climbing plants such as sweet peas or beans can be grown on trellis-work against a wall. Discussion can centre on their method of climbing and children's attention can be drawn to other climbing plants such as ivy, blackberry and convolvulus. Lots of statistics might result.

How many flowers on a single plant?
How many fruits?
How many seeds?

Children could, for example, collect a lot of peapods.

How many pods have no seeds?
How many have one seed?
How many have two seeds, etc?

Soil   Paving stone

A chequer-board garden

The results make an interesting graph.

Growing things will inevitably lead to the consideration of soils (and things associated with soils) and to watering.

Watering

Using the right sort of apparatus to carry out watering children can learn a lot about water itself. At a simple level the apparatus might consist of cans with a single hole or a number of holes in the base that are dipped into a bucket of water and the water then sprinkled over the plants.

What happens if you keep putting your finger on and off the hole in the lid?

A garden hose is very useful. How far can the stream of water go? What happens if the hole at the end of the hose is partially closed with a single finger? What happens if it is a windy day? Can children get the stream of water from the hose to hit a target?

It is possible for each child to make his own stream using a squeezy bottle with the fine nozzle replaced after filling.

How far can a stream be shot before it breaks up?

What ways can be devised of measuring this distance? How does the tilt of the squeezy bottle affect the length of the stream? What effect does squeezing the bottle hard have on the length of the stream? What happens to streams when they meet?

What happens to a stream on a smooth or a rough piece of timber, a sloping playground or a window-pane? On which of these surfaces does it hold together? Where does it break up?

Try shooting an unbroken stream of water into a bucket of water. Now try a stream that is breaking into drops. Is there any difference in sound?

Soils

What does soil feel like? Infants will find that a sandy soil is gritty and runs through their hands fairly easily whilst a clay soil is heavier, stickier and will bind more easily. Clay soil is ideal for them to make small bricks which they can bake in the sun (see page 90).

What words can children find to describe the *feel*

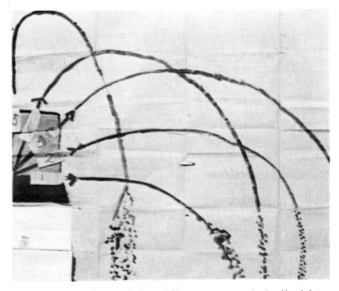

of various soils and the differences and similarities they find between one soil and another? How quickly do different soils settle when stirred in water? What patterns do they form in the jar? What effect do different tools have on soil?

Try digging, hoeing and raking. Is this effect different if the soil is wet?

Footprints
Shoes will leave imprints on the soil surface.

51

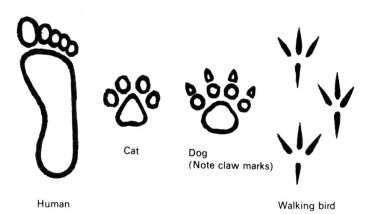

Make a plaster cast of one.

Roll a strip of card to form a circle.

Hold in place with paper-clips and put around the footprint.

Pour plaster of Paris of the right consistency into the centre of the card and allow it to set.

Experiment with mixes to find which is best. Brush away any soil adhering to the hardened cast with an old toothbrush.

Make casts of a child's footprint and of footprints of other animals such as cats, dogs and birds.

Human   Cat   Dog
                          (Note claw marks)   Walking bird

Things that turn up

What comes from the soil? Mostly pebbles and stones but often lots of other things—perhaps an empty snail shell, some seeds, partly decayed plant material and lots of animals. Sort and discuss them. Look at a few of the animals that will probably turn up in more detail.

Snails
Keep some snails in an old aquarium. Put some damp soil in the base and keep it moist. The snails will feed on greenery and oats rolled in crushed chalk.

Is there a pattern on the snail shell? Children might look around for other snails. Are they all alike? Do they all have the same pattern on their shells? Where are the snails eyes? Infants love to touch them (gently). What happens?

The snail moves on a single foot. Place it in a jam jar or on the side of an empty aquarium and watch the rhythmical contractions of the muscles in the foot as the animal moves. Snails can move at a surprising pace and it is often easy to have a snail race. How long did the winner take to cover the track?

What do snails feed on? With fresh-water snails in an aquarium it is easy for the children to see the long file-like tongue scraping algae off the side of the tank. Can children see what the snails breathe through?

Woodlice
Woodlice are very common in damp places, especially under stones. Collect some.

They can be kept for a short time in a transparent sandwich box.

Line the bottom with damp blotting paper and put in some stones and bark for them to shelter under.

They will feed on chopped-up bits of potato.

Damp blotting paper

What shape are they? Look not only at their general shape from front to rear but also their cross-sectional shape or shape from top to bottom. Are they all the same size?

What colour are they? Does it help them to merge with their background?

How many segments do they have? How many legs? What do they feel with?

What surfaces can they walk on? Try a stone, a ruler, a piece of wood, paper, a plastic sandwich box. Will they walk up slopes?

Do they really like damp places? Test this out with a plastic sandwich box with damp blotting paper at one end. Where do they tend to congregate?

Earthworms
What shape is an earthworm? How does it move? Does burrowing involve a lot of work? Children can make their own surface burrows in a piece of ground using garden trowels.

How does an earthworm burrow? Earthworms eat their way through the soil using their muscles to pull them forward and bristles on their undersurface to grip the soil. Put an earthworm on a piece of brown paper, hold the paper near an ear and listen. The scratching of the bristles on the surface of the paper will be clearly heard. Watch the earthworm moving. Does it move

faster on paper than on the soil surface?

Draw the children's attention to worm casts or to leaves sticking upright from the mouth of a burrow.

A temporary home can be quickly improvised from a large jam jar. Dampen the soil before you put it in the jar, not afterwards, or you will destroy the crumb structure of the soil.

If the jar is covered with black paper for some days and this is then removed, burrows will probably be seen against the side of the jar.

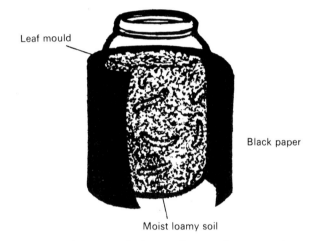

Leaf mould

Black paper

Moist loamy soil

There is a lot more information and suggestions about small animals in the Project's publication *Minibeasts.*

Here are just three animals. Many more will turn up. Try and get children to pose questions about them and to find answers. Once an animal is taken indoors many more ideas may arise. For example:

Can an earthworm hear noises?

What is the biggest gap between two books that it will cross?

Once children become trained in this way of thinking the questions will pose themselves.

Cooking things

There are many experiences of a scientific nature that children can gain from cooking things. Cooking also provides opportunities for weighing and costing, gives material for written work and entails discussion and thus extension of vocabulary. Children learn to work together, take turns and gain much pleasure from their tasks and a regard for simple hygiene. Cooking also gives opportunities for the less able child, as one teacher said, 'My best pastry maker is one of my slowest children'. The following recipes are chosen because they contain a number of experiences of a *scientific* nature.

Some recipes

Shortbread

Ingredients
225 g [8 oz] flour
115 g [4 oz] butter
55 g [2 oz] castor sugar
$\frac{1}{4}$ teaspoon salt

Method
The butter is softened in a mixing bowl. Flour and salt are sieved into the bowl and sugar is added. These ingredients are then rubbed together with the tips of the fingers until they are well mixed in. The mixture is kneaded until it forms a ball and is then pressed evenly into a greased flat tin with a blunt knife. It is pricked with a fork and placed in the oven at 350°F for thirty minutes.

When cool the shortbread is cut into fingers in the tin.

Some six-year-olds doing this began to experience the pliability of materials and their ability to mix with one another. They found, for example, that butter softened more quickly in their hands than when mixed with a spoon. They also noted how their mixture came away more cleanly from the sides of the china basin than from the sides of the plastic bowls and saw how the shortbread cooked fastest at the top of the oven. They discussed why this happened. Some children put in too much sugar and found that their shortbread was very hard. Another group discussed the keeping qualities of shortbread and this led them to talking about staleness and freshness of food.

Why do biscuits go soggy out of a tin?

What is *bad* food?

What ways can food be kept?

Bread

Ingredients
1360 g [3 lb] plain flour
3-7 level teaspoons salt
710 cm³ [1$\frac{1}{4}$ pints] warm water
30 g [1 oz] yeast
1-2 level teaspoons sugar
30 g [1 oz] lard or margarine (this is rubbed into flour and helps to keep the bread moist)

Method
Put the flour and salt through a sieve into a warm basin. Mix the yeast and sugar in another basin and add a little of the warm water. Make a well in the centre of the flour and pour the liquid into it. Give a light dusting of flour over the top, cover with a

cloth and leave in a warm place for about fifteen minutes until the top is covered with bubbles.

Knead the dough until it is smooth and leaves the sides of the bowl clean. Leave it for about one and a half hours to rise and then knead again. Feel it. One five-year-old who did this remarked, 'It feels like my puppy's tummy. Is it alive?'

Form the dough into leaves and put it into warmed and lightly greased bread tins, half filling them. Leave the dough again for about twenty minutes.

Bake in the centre of a hot oven (425-450°F or Mark 6-7) for ten minutes. Reduce the heat to 375°F or Mark 4 for a further thirty to forty-five minutes depending on the size of the loaves.

Test the loaves by knocking on the bottom. They should sound hollow when ready. Leave to cool.

Alternatively children can make a very small loaf each.

Yeast acts on sugar to produce a gas (carbon dioxide) which causes the bread to rise.

Something of the nature of this action can be observed by putting yeast into a bottle containing a strong solution of sugar and leaving the bottle in a warm place.

The yeast, feeding on the sugar, gives off so much gas that a great deal of froth will rise in the bottle (allow some hours for this to occur).

Try making a small amount of bread without yeast. How does the texture of this compare with normal bread? Why is one porous and the other not? What happens to bread made with yeast that has been mixed with boiling water? What has the heat done to the yeast?

This work led one class of five-year-olds to looking at pictures of wheat, rye and barley;

a combine harvester; a biblical picture of Mary grinding corn; pictures of windmills; and to collecting pictures of different kinds of bread.

Lightly corked

Water, sugar and yeast

Ginger beer

Ingredients
2 lemons
30 g [1 oz] bruised root ginger
225 g [8 oz] sugar
15 g [½ oz] cream of tartar
15 g [½ oz] yeast on toast
4·5 l [1 gall] cold water

Method
Put the rinds of the lemons, ginger, cream of tartar, sugar and water in a large saucepan or boiler and bring to the boil. Leave until lukewarm and then float the raft of toast bearing the yeast on the mixture. Cover with a cloth and stand for twenty-four hours.

Strain, bottle and store in a cool place. It should be ready for drinking in two to three days.

Here again yeast is acting on sugar but in this case the gas given off in the action is trapped as bubbles in the beer. It might be interesting to make up the mixture but omit the yeast. How does this mixture compare with ginger beer made with yeast? How does it taste?

Butter

Ingredients
190 cm³ [⅓ pint] of cream (top of the milk)
Salt to taste

Method
Take the top of the milk from several bottles of milk and put it in a screw-top jar. Shake the jar until the cream turns to butter.

Children will need to take turns and the process often takes some time. The liquid left in the jar is called buttermilk. Taste it.

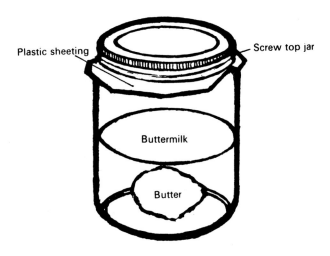

Add salt to the butter and beat it with a fork. How much butter comes from the cream ? How long did it take to make the butter ?

One class listed their preferences for salted and unsalted butter.

If possible butter might be made from ordinary milk, Jersey milk and Guernsey milk. How do the different butters compare ?

The whole process of making butter might be approached by asking, 'I wonder what will happen if we shake milk in a jar ?' What suggestions have children for naming the substance that forms ?

56

Salted butter was the most popular.

	Salted	Unsalted	Do not know
14	Mary		
13	Maude		
12	June R		
11	Susan	Tog	
10	NIGLA	Paul	
9	John	Neil	
8	Bernard	Roger	
7	SHARON	A LAN	
6	Elaine	Helen	
5	Paul	PAUL	David
4	Roger	Moon	Leat
3	Gary	Andrew	
2	PHILIP	Kim	Sharon
1	James	Brian	Nikki

Which butter is the more popular ?

Cheese

Ingredients
Unpasteurised milk (obtained from a dairy)

Method
Keep a bottle of unpasteurised milk in a warm place for a couple of days until it goes sour. Set the sour milk to drain through muslin overnight.

By the next day the *whey* will have drained into the basin leaving the *curds,* which have changed to cottage cheese, in the muslin.

This will be an early experience of filtering for many children—the solid remaining in the muslin, the liquid running through into the basin. One class who did this had a long discussion about the foods that came from milk and talked about yoghurt, cheese, cream, butter and junket.

Dehydrated foods
Soak prunes, apricots, peas and so on. What happens ? What dried foods can the children bring to form a class collection ?

Meringues

Ingredients
2 whites of egg
115 g [4 oz] castor sugar
Pinch of salt

Method
Separate whites of egg from yolks. Put whites in a basin with a pinch of salt and beat them with a

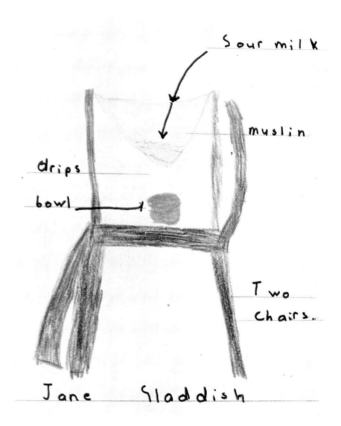

whisk until they stand up in the bowl. What does it taste like ?

Put in half the sugar. Taste again. (Might be the point at which to discuss different sugars.)

Mix very carefully and then add all the sugar and beat lightly. Put teaspoonfuls of the mixture on a greased baking tray and cook for two hours at 200°F.

Scientific experiences gained from cooking

Dissolving, stirring, evaporation
Children find some substances will *dissolve.* This might be extended to finding out and listing all the

soluble and *insoluble* substances they can find.

Stirring helps substances dissolve. When making bread, for example, there might be two groups dissolving sugar. If one stirs and the other does not which group gets its sugar to dissolve quickest ? Does warm water help the dissolving ?

Can dissolved substances be retrieved ? A little sugar solution in a saucer can be set over a radiator to evaporate. Taste the retrieved 'grains', sometimes these are not even visible and you have to wet your finger and rub it on the saucer to pick up some sugar.

Often during cooking water is spilled. Here perhaps is an opportunity to introduce the word liquid. Children might later list all the other liquids such as milk, squash, coffee, tea, lemonade, cooking oil, petrol and so on, that they can think of.

Duration of events
How long must the cakes be in the oven ? What time were they put in ? What time must they be taken out ? If the kitchen staff are loaning their cooker at what time must the children present themselves ?

Changes in substances
A fat can change to an oil. Milk turns sour. Butter comes from milk. The white of an egg becomes stiff as air is beaten into it.

Heating things
Heating brings about a profound change in ingredients. Here the idea of reversibility takes form—it is not possible to take bread and get back all the ingredients one started with. Infants will also come across the need to regulate temperature.

Use of tools
The effects of kitchen implements such as beaters, whips, mincers and graters can be noted. A beater often employs a large wheel to turn smaller wheels, children can note how this does work for them.

How many turns of the small wheel do they get for one turn of the large wheel ? Can they think of other places where wheels are used in this way ?

Cleanliness
Its importance can be discussed and linked with the harmful effect of germs.

Material existing in more than one form
Sugar, for example, exists in lump, granulated, rock and powdered form. Collect as many different sugars as you can.

Measuring
Volume, capacity, weighing, and measuring are an integral part of activities associated with cooking. Some six and seven-year-olds making chocolate crunchies, for example, were surprised at the difference in bulk between a 2oz [50 g] weight and 2 oz [50 g] of cornflakes.

Smelling

One usually associates smell and taste with cooking. Young children find it difficult to describe smells. Mostly they use an analogy 'it smells like a flower', 'it smells like cooking'. Chance remarks on smell often come during an outdoor walk—from wet soil, fresh mown grass, flowers, tar, petrol, exhaust fumes, industrial smells and, of course, a farmyard has smells all its own.

Children might bring things to make a class display of materials with a smell :

orange	moth balls	chopped hay
apple	smelling salts	pine needles
ripe banana	bath salts	flowers
onion	perfume	spices
cheese	a pot-pourri	

Let them sniff. Many children blow when told to sniff and you'll have to teach them how to do it. Which smell do you like best ?

Can you classify smells?

Discussion might see the introduction of words such as flowery, 'high', rotten, spicy, sharp; or a consideration of the smells children associate with home (wax on the floor, a casserole cooking, mummy's scent).

Stopping smells
Collect something with a strong smell such as cheese or moth balls. How could you stop the smell reaching you? Try holding your nose!
Try putting things in a plastic bag or air-tight box. What else can you think to do?

A guessing game
Some of the substances children bring for their *smelling* table can be put in a series of boxes or beakers and each container covered with muslin. Can children guess what is in each box by smell alone? Make a chart listing their correct guesses. (See page 60.)

Noses
What are noses of different animals like? Look at the classroom pets. Can they move their noses?

A class of six-year-olds made models of noses in Plasticine, they ranged from a child's nose to that of an elephant. This led to a discussion of the accentuated sense of smell blind people have and how herb gardens are planted for them.

Smell and taste
There is a link between smell and taste. Blindfold a child. Hold his nose firmly and put a piece of food into his mouth. Can he guess what it is? Children sometimes guess what the food is by its texture on the tongue but it is often difficult to tell until the grip on the nose is released. Try carrot, potato, tomato, cheese, onion and so on.

Tasting

A *tasting* table on which a range of food is set out for children to taste can be fun. Do they like all the things they taste? Which foods do they like best? Block graphs might be drawn showing individual preferences.

There are four basic tastes: sweet, salt, sour, bitter. Whilst this point need not be laboured with young children it is useful to include examples of these tastes:

sweet honey, sugar
salt
sour lemon, sour pickles, grapefruit rind
bitter instant coffee, cooking chocolate

In addition there are foods with a combination of flavours: sweet pickles, lemon drops and apples are both sweet and sour. Peanut butter is sweet and salty.

Visiting the sweetshop
Visit the sweetshop. How many different flavours can you buy for 5p? Is there a close link between colour and flavour? Make a block chart showing individual preferences in a packet of fruit gums.

The children can soak some of the sweets in water. Some, especially sherbet fizzers, will dissolve much more quickly than others. Which sweets retain their colour in water? Which sweets lose their colour in water?

Flavouring water
Children find this fun. Discuss ways to do it. Squash, lemonade powder, Oxo, jelly and fruit salts are safe to use.

Making jelly is an especially good way of linking colour and smell and, of course, dissolving and gelation come up.

One infant was interested in the transparency of jellies and this led to a collection of things that could be seen through. (See page 73.)

Children like to discuss their favourite foods. There are also some lovely colours. How about a red and yellow jelly, a pink blancmange and a (yellow) custard.

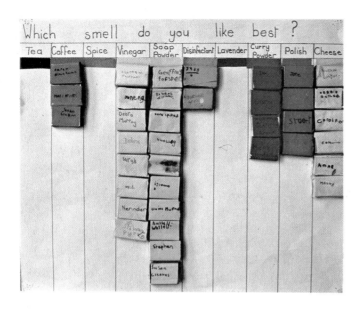

Which smell do you like best?

Tea	Coffee	Spice	Vinegar	Soap Powder	Disinfectant	Lavender	Curry Powder	Polish	Cheese

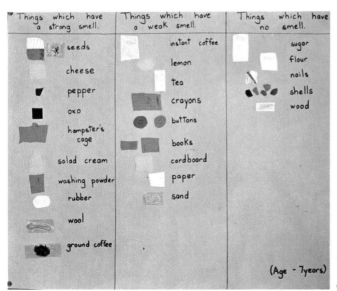

Things which have a strong smell.	Things which have a weak smell.	Things which have no smell.
seeds	instant coffee	sugar
cheese	lemon	flour
pepper	tea	nails
oxo	crayons	shells
hampster's cage	buttons	wood
salad cream	books	
washing powder	cardboard	
rubber	paper	
wool	sand	
ground coffee		

(Age - 7years)

This chart came from the guessing game on page 59

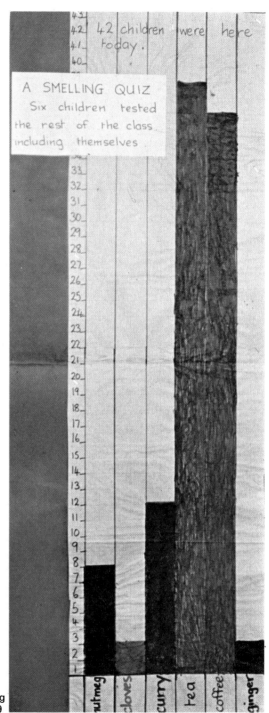

42 children were here today.

A SMELLING QUIZ
Six children tested the rest of the class including themselves

nutmeg	cloves	curry	tea	coffee	ginger

60

The cows are being milked

Coconut
Cones

Karen
Kevin
Helen
Angela

Class 1

Making a Christmas cake

61

Looking after things

Animals

What educational possibilities lie within the field of looking after animals? When infants handle a pet, attention and discussion can centre on shape, body covering, weight, movement, breathing, heartbeat.

Shape and appearance
Noticing the shape of an animal often tells a great deal about its way of moving. A fish, a bird and a frog are streamlined for moving through water or the air; a rabbit and a squirrel have powerful curved hindlimbs for hopping; guinea-pigs and hamsters are squat and compact, well adapted for moving on land. How does a streamlined shape help movement? (See 'Boats' page 22.)

An animal's body may be covered with hair, fur, scales or feathers which protect it and keep it warm. Children might investigate this body covering. Which will cool most quickly, a tin full of warm water or a tin full of warm water surrounded by a fur muff?

What shape are the limbs of each animal? How many toes are there? How are the toes used for grasping things? For example:

How does a hamster hold a piece of apple?
How does a budgerigar grasp its perch?

Where are the eyes placed?
How wide a field of vision is there?

What shape are the ears of various animals?
How can their ears catch sounds?

What does an animal sense food with?

Behaviour
Moving
How does an animal move? Does it push against anything? A rabbit has large hind feet for pushing against the ground or burrowing; fish use certain fins for rising and descending in the water, for moving forward and for maintaining their position. Can the children tell which are used for each task? Birds hop or walk or run, in the air they may fly in a straight line or in short bursts or with an undulating pattern. A water bird such as a duck has broad paddles for pushing against the water.

Move your hands in water in a sink or bowl with fingers open and fingers closed.

How much push is there?

Where do you experience the greatest push?

Does this tell you anything about the way a frog or a duck swims? Collect pictures of different animals and discuss the way they move.

Here is a good example of observation by a six-year-old:

'Today I brought my stick insect's old skin that he had shed. It was about 3 cm long. He is grey but the skin is white. Yesterday I looked at my stick insect's jar, I saw something white, I thought he was dead, but he was not dead. It was his old skin. His old skin is hard. His new skin is soft. He feels funny. Today I brought my stick insect to school. His grip feels horrid. His feet seem as if they are magnetic. They could curl round the leaf.

Today I could not see my stick insect because he looked exactly like a stick. When I hit the jar he dropped down looking dead.'

Sensing things

Which organs are sensitive to touch, light, sound, smell, taste ? How do pets respond to sudden sounds ? How do they sense danger ? Is there parental care ?

Bring a kitten to school for the day, it will stimulate much talking and, perhaps, recording.

Pull a paper ball along on a string in front of the kitten. How does the kitten respond to the ball ?

Can the children spot what things will help the kitten catch food when it is older ? What sounds does it make as it scratches at a window-pane, drinks milk or just lies contented ? One class tried a kitten with several kinds of food. It went for the fish. They tried it with a saucer of milk and a saucer of water. It preferred the milk. Which foods do the children's pets prefer ? Which foods are not very popular ? Which do they dislike ?

Try listing pets under the following headings.

How much push is there on water ?

Milk	Water	Nuts	Corn	Greenery	Meat	etc

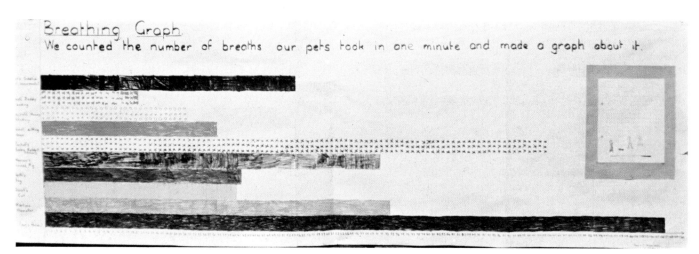

Breathing Graph
We counted the number of breaths our pets took in one minute and made a graph about it.

Do animals respond to colour? Try placing bowls of food for the birds on different coloured backgrounds.

Breathing
Watch a fish in the aquarium. Note the opening and closing of the gill cover as water passes over the gills. Why does the gill cover open and close? How many times does the gill cover move in a minute? How many times does the gill cover move in a minute if the fish has been disturbed?

Measuring things
Amount of food
How much food do pets eat? How much water do they drink?

Put a scale against a budgerigar's food hopper and mark off the daily food intake.

What methods can you devise for doing this with other school pets?

How accurate do you think they are?

Weight
How does the weight of an animal increase with time? Weigh a guinea-pig daily against any arbitrary measure such as small nails. It is best to start with a young animal.

Some six-year-olds made a simple balance from a coat-hanger with plastic egg-cups suspended from it, and weighed a moth against melon pips. They recorded their results by sticking the requisite number of pips for each daily weighing on to a large sheet of paper making a series of vertical columns. There was a gradual increase in weight and then one day a sudden drop—the moth had laid eggs.

Number of animals
How many birds visit the bird table in an hour? What birds are they?

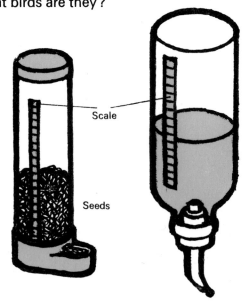

Scale

Seeds

How many earthworms can children find when they dig their garden plot?

How many animals are there under a large stone?

How many kinds of animals are present?

How many are there of each kind?

Such investigations will naturally link up with the way animals move, feed and breathe.

Habits
Draw attention to wild animals, especially birds.

Do these animals live a solitary life or are they social creatures? Does the animal have a territory? (The robin is a good example of a bird with its own domain.)

What enemies do these animals have? How do they avoid them? What are their daily activities?

Reference books
Two books that deal with the housing and care of animals are:

Animals and Plants, Nuffield Junior Science, Collins.

Animals in Schools, J. P. Volrath, John Murray for University Federation of Animal Welfare.

A useful background booklet is:

Mammals in Classrooms, Nuffield Junior Science, Collins.

Ourselves

What is entailed in looking after ourselves?

Washing
What helps remove grease and dirt from the body? Try water, water and soap, warm water and soap. Which is best?

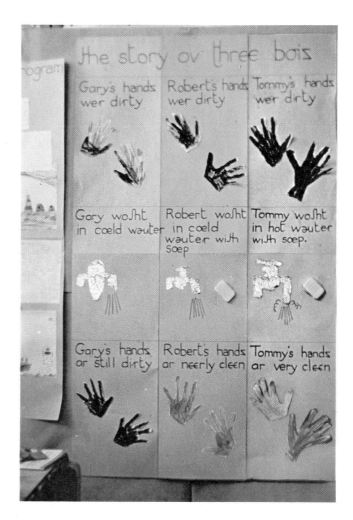

What else can be used? Bath salts, washing-up liquid, liquid soap, shampoo, soap flakes—what effect do all these substances produce? How much lather can be got from a teaspoonful of each of these substances? Is it only fair to use the same amount of water in each case? Lots of bubbles result.

A digression on bubbles
How many ways can children find of making bubbles? Try clapping hands in water, moving containers about in water, squeezing a plastic bottle or sponge or a large cloth under water; blowing down a pipe or drinking straw into

water, or blowing up a balloon and letting the air out under water.

Can you control the size of bubbles? Can you find a way to produce a constant stream of bubbles? (A strong soap solution (washing-up liquid dissolved in water) and bubble pipes or pieces of wire bent into circles are ideal for blowing bubbles.)

What makes the best bubbles? Try detergents, shampoo, bath salts, washing powders. Does it make a difference if you add the water to the washing-up liquid or the washing-up liquid to the water?

What shape are bubbles? What shape are the bubbles in the water? What happens to a bubble when it hits the floor? Look closely. Where else can children find bubbles? (In an aquarium, a spirit level.)

What colours are the bubbles when viewed against a dark background?

A corked, 60-cm length of plastic tube is useful. How do bubbles travel along it?

Put some beads in and watch them travel through the water.

Try making bubble patterns by blowing down a drinking straw into a large jar of soapy water. Add some powder paint to water and washing-up liquid in a shallow bowl. Blow into the mixture until you get a mass of coloured bubbles standing up in the bowl. Invert a sheet of paper over the bubbles. What sort of patterns do you get?

Brushing teeth
Where especially does food stick to teeth? Look at teeth in a mirror. What shape are they? How many teeth are there? Some have sharp edges, like chisels, and are used for biting; others have four points on them (feel with a finger) and are used for chewing. How many of each are there?

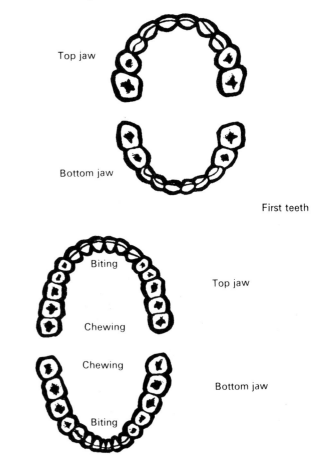

66

Bite into a clean piece of Plasticine and get an impression of your teeth. If a ridge is formed around the 'plate', plaster of Paris can be poured in and a cast formed. (See page 52 for a method of making plaster casts.)

Which is the best way to clean teeth? Children might try finding an answer to this using an old set of dentures and a toothbrush. The false teeth can be smeared with a mixture of wet sand and then brushed. Children will soon realise that it is easier to get all the grains out by brushing up and down between the teeth rather than across them.

What sort of teeth do the children's pets have? What food do these animals eat?

Keeping warm
How do we keep warm? Some children suggested 'fires', 'by rubbing hands', 'putting a coat on'. Discuss how to keep warm in summer and in winter.

Put several coats on. What do you feel like after five minutes? Of the clothes you wear which are thinnest? thickest? warmest? Dress some dolls made from squeezy bottles in different clothes.

Cardboard heads

Wrapped in fur

Wrapped in a tea towel

Knitted suit

Wrapped in kitchen foil—a spaceman

Fill them all with hot water at the same time. Which cools first? Feel each doll (under its 'clothes') after about an hour. Which feels warmest? Which feels coldest? What does this tell us about the material covering them?

Make some cardboard dolls dressed according to season. Dress some dolls in the costume of different lands. Is there a relationship with climate.

Regular sleep
Discuss the importance of regular sleep. Make a bedtime graph, perhaps from matchboxes, showing the number who go to bed at 6.30 pm, 7 pm, 7.30 pm and so on. Is the graph for a weekday night the same as that for a Saturday night?

What about getting up? Who gets up earliest?

Washing things

Clothes
Wash some dolls' clothes or pieces of rag that are suitably dirty in cold water, cold water plus soap flakes, warm water and warm water plus soap flakes. Where do you get the best results?

Try a range of washing powders and soaps. Collect rainwater in a bucket and wash some clothes in it. What effect does it have?

Similar activities may be carried out on dishes and pots and pans from the Wendy house. Such activity can often be followed up with an investigation of drying things (see page 87).

Windows
Clean a window with a dry sponge, a wet sponge, a wet soapy sponge, a dry chamois leather and a damp chamois leather. Where do you get the best results?

On warm sunny days we wear thin cool clothes.

On cold cloudy days we wear thick warm clothes.

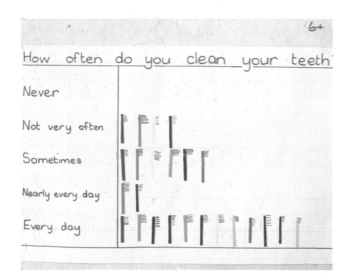

How often do you clean your teeth

Never

Not very often

Sometimes

Nearly every day

Every day

6+

we have made a graph about
looking after your teeth exactly half of
the children clen there teeth
every day and exacely half do not
we look at the twelve childrens
teeth they were white
I think it is sensible to clen
your teeth every day
most of the children who clen
there teeth Every day have
nice white ones

Painted things

List all the painted things children see on a walk. Walls, drainpipes, woodwork, railings and so on may figure. Why are things painted?

For effect	A mural to brighten up a dull wall
To convey information	A. Smith, Greengrocer Bloggs Tyres are Best
To protect things	Metals against corrosion Woods against decay
To act as a warning	Road traffic signs

Metals

What happens to unpainted metal? Note all the places where rusting occurs. How many rusty objects can children collect to make a display? What have all the rusty objects got in common? How can rust be removed?

Try emery paper or sand-paper. Will rusty objects that have been cleaned with emery paper rust again? Try putting one on a shelf in the classroom, one buried in the soil, another half buried in the soil and one outdoors on a window sill. Leave them for a fortnight—it is hoped that it rains during that time.

Do any parts of the children's tricycles rust?

Wood

Where can children find unpainted wood outdoors? What does it look like? Is there anything growing on it?

Worn-out things

What sort of things wear out? Make a collection. It might include the sole of a shoe, a brake block from a bicycle, trousers with a hole in them, a pencil stub, a rubber, a tyre, a paintbrush.

Where can you find things that are worn away

Cleaning a rusty hinge with emery paper. Will it rust again if left outdoors?

Will a tin can rust if it is buried in the soil?

around the school? Perhaps worn steps, paint off a hand-rail or a groove worn in a slide.

Children asked for an explanation will probably suggest 'rubbing'. They might list all the things worn away by *friction* and discuss how these could be replaced or repaired.

Looking after a tricycle

Try and get a boy living near the school to bring his tricycle. It is also useful to borrow some spanners and an oil-can.

Are the handlebars at a comfortable height?

How can they be adjusted?

Is the seat at a suitable height? How can it be adjusted?

Are the brakes working properly? Are the brake blocks worn? What causes this? How can they be replaced?

Are the tyres worn? What causes this? Are the pedals worn? What causes this? Is the reflector clear?

Are the wheels steady? Are they oiled? Why do we oil them? Is the bell working? Does it need oiling? What else can children find (both at home and at school) that needs oiling?

Looking at things

Looking around

Eyes

'I spy' might be a good place to begin. 'I spy with my little eye something big, round, red.' What shapes can children spy?

How many eyes are there in the classroom? What colours are they? How many eyes are there of each colour? Make a block graph.

What stops you seeing?—night, closing eyes, hands over eyes, fog. Light is necessary in order to see things.

Can you find your way across the classroom with eyes closed?

Can you guess what various objects placed in your hand are, if you are blindfolded?

Can you guess what various objects in a shoe-bag are by touch alone?

Can you recognise your friends by touch only?

Other animals' eyes

Where are the eyes in animals? Dogs and cats have them at the front of their heads. These animals hunt for prey.

Rabbits have eyes at the sides of their heads for they need to keep a wary eye out for predators; they therefore need a wide field of vision. Older infants may appreciate this, for one six-year-old, when asked, 'Why do you think animals' eyes are at the side?' replied, 'So that they can run away'. When asked, 'Why?' she replied, 'Because they can see sooner'.

One group of children made masks of animals' heads with holes for eyes in order to control the way the children could look out.

What about fish? Look at them in the aquarium, how wide a field of vision do children think these have? Do they have eyelids?

Look at school pets, such as hamsters, guinea-pigs and mice. Do insects, spiders, snails, slugs, woodlice and worms have eyes? Collect pictures showing animals' eyes.

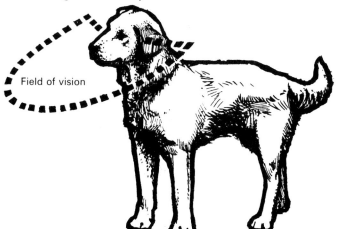

Field of vision

Position of view

How do things look from different viewpoints? One class discussed looking at things from a bird's-eye view, a moving plane, the top of a Big Wheel, lying flat and looking at 'mouse's-eye level' and looking through a very small hole.

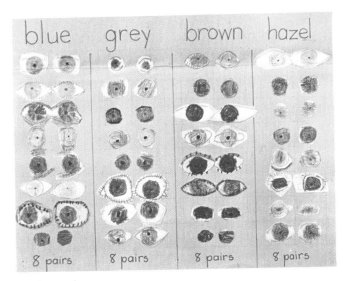

Eyes in our class

Colours

Indoors

What colours can be found in the classroom?
Make lists of objects under colour headings.
(Children will probably find they need a special
category for objects with more than one colour.)
What is the predominant colour in the classroom?
Which colour occurs most times in the
classroom? Which colour is your favourite?
Which colour can you see most clearly down the
classroom?

What colours and shades of colour can be got
by mixing paints? What happens if you mix two
colours? What happens if you mix three colours?
Who can make the greatest range of colours? Who

Laura

My cat's eyes are green
With Black pupils in
there middle and at night
rheire eyes light up and
make green light In the
dark and at day rime
rhey are nearly closed
But rhey can see.

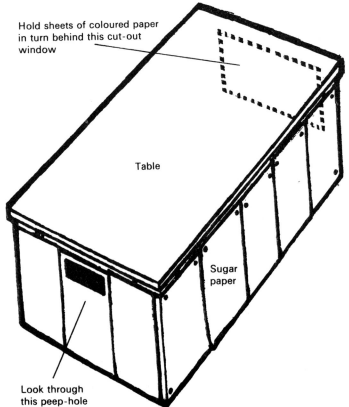

Hold sheets of coloured paper
in turn behind this cut-out
window

Table

Sugar
paper

Look through
this peep-hole

can produce the most shades of grey ? What must be done in order to get shades of colour ?

How many different coloured drinks can you make ? How many different things can you find to colour water ? Put a range of coloured liquids on a side window where they can catch the light.

What colours can you see in the dark ?

Outdoors
What colours are to be found outdoors ? Make lists of all the places where man uses colours. Draw attention to use of colour :

For effect	Tiles on a roof
In paints	To convey information eg A. J. Smith, Greengrocer For protection (see page 69)
As a warning	Road traffic signs

What colours are all the cars in a car park ? Sort them according to colour or shade of colour. Children find variation in shades of green fascinating, they might use them to make an attractive collage. Can some colours, for example, those painted on a wall or in a poster, be seen for greater distances than others ? If the sun goes in does it have an effect on the colours ?

Who sees best of a group of children ? Try drawing a small picture about 5 cm², sticking it with Sellotape to a wall and letting the children advance until they recognise it. Each child stops as soon as he thinks he can identify the picture. How far is each child from the picture before he recognises it ? Plot these distances on a graph.

Looking through things

Transparent objects
Collect transparent objects. Bottles, tumblers, jam jars, plastic wrapping, plastic food boxes, spectacles, an aquarium and so on. Is it easy to see through *all* the objects in the collection ? How many layers of polythene can you see through ?

A new plastic bag is easy to see through but it loses it transparency with age. The same applies to a plastic lunch box. If children look closely they will see tiny scratches on the box which scatter the light and affect its transparency.

Grease and dirt also affect transparency of objects. How can these be removed ? (See pages 65 and 67.)

What do things look like in water ? What other liquids can you see through ?

Transparent objects

Translucent and opaque objects
What must you look at objects through for them to appear blurred ? Some children said reeded glass and a vase, one boy said 'my shirt'. What things cannot be seen through ?

Lenses
Collect lenses from old spectacles, a telescope or a magnifying glass. Children often say these have a bump in the middle. Look through them. Sometimes an enlarged image is seen. What else magnifies ? A round vinegar bottle full of water will act as a magnifier.

Do not forget that large magnifiers of the Sherlock Holmes type are essential in the infant classroom.

What effect do the water drops have on the size of the newsprint?

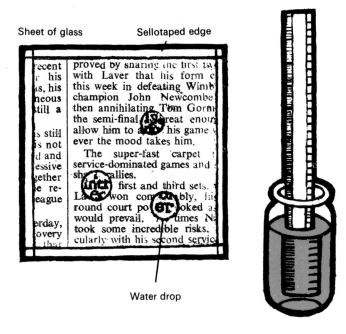

Sheet of glass   Sellotaped edge

Water drop

As well as affecting the apparent size of an object a lens can throw an image.

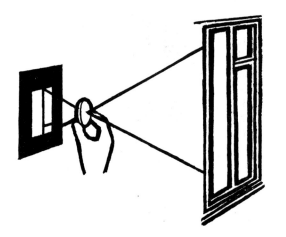

Children looking through telescopes and binoculars will realise how the lenses both enlarge objects and appear to bring them nearer. What do they see if they look through the 'wrong' end of a telescope?

Looking in things

Reflections
What can you see yourself in? Some children said 'mirrors', 'my mum's ashtray', 'a clock face' and 'somebody else's eyes'. Puddles, windows, ponds, plate-glass doorways, an aquarium and most metallic objects give reflections.

Collect objects that give reflections. List all the places where infants see themselves reflected. What is your image like in a mirror, the front of a spoon, the back of a spoon, a stainless steel teapot?

Mirrors
Provide plenty of handbag mirrors, they are inexpensive and ideal for use in the classroom. Inevitably they get broken and it is useful to cover the back of them with Sellotape so that broken pieces can be easily disposed of.

What does writing look like in a mirror?

Can you draw a picture on a piece of paper whilst looking only in a mirror? Can you invent a shield to prevent 'cheating'? Where does a mirror have to be held to see, behind? overhead? round a corner?

Use a mirror outdoors to reflect the sun's rays (the same effect can be got indoors with a torch).

Reflect a spot of light from a mirror:

How far can the spot go? Can it be shone into the shade? On to the ground? Can it be shone into the sunlight? What shape is the spot? Always?

Play a game chasing one another's 'spots'. Do the spots get mixed up or is it easy to follow one's own spot?

One six-year-old child brought a concave shaving mirror to school—the images obtained in this caused much amusement. What are the images in a concave mirror like?

Toys and mirrors
Place an object between two mirrors facing one another.

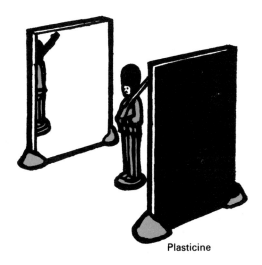

Plasticine

Look down the side of one mirror into the other.

Can you see a succession of receding images?

Can you count them?

Place two mirrors at an angle with an object between them.

How many images are there?

How many images if the angle between the two mirrors is varied?

This principle is embodied in a kaleidoscope. Look through a kaleidoscope.

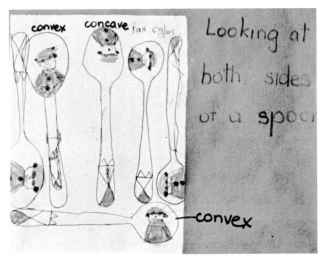

This is fun. What else can we find that is convex or concave?

A six-year-old's drawing of a child viewed through a magnifying sheet

Looking through a magnifying sheet

76

Claire Evans 18th march

Why I wear a pony tail

MµY I Meah a bout a bou tail

mirror writing

When I look at writing in a mirror it is upside down and back to front and it looks funny.

Can you see through jelly?

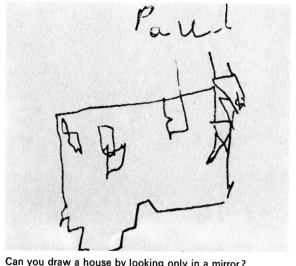

Paul

Can you draw a house by looking only in a mirror?

Periscopes

Try making some as shown in the diagrams.

Of course some adult help is needed here.

Two wooden wedges for gluing the mirrors to are easily obtained by cutting diagonally across a wooden cube.

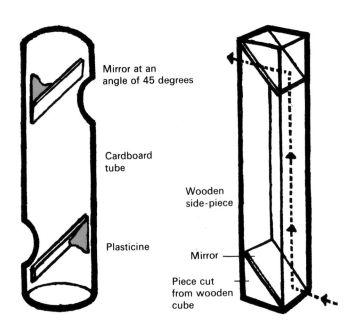

Mirror at an angle of 45 degrees

Cardboard tube

Plasticine

Wooden side-piece

Mirror

Piece cut from wooden cube

Looking at areas

Often children look at a particular area in some detail. Much of this looking results in direct discussion and questioning, either amongst themselves with the teachers or with other adults. Often something to do arises. Let us look at some areas where experiences of a scientific nature may occur.

Looking at a building site

Digging trenches and laying foundations

Talk to the workmen and handle their tools. How does a workman use a pick? Why does it enter the ground so easily? Why does he spit on his hands before catching hold of the pick handle?

Feel how smooth the handle is. Where do you get the best grip on a smooth dry handle or a smooth wet handle?

How does the workman lever on his spade? (Let the children try digging in the school garden. How do they hold their spades to get a shovel full of soil easily?)

Look at the foundations. They will probably be made with concrete. Children like making their own concrete bricks (see page 90). Why are foundations necessary? Children might 'feel' an answer to this by pressing a broomstick handle on soft ground and then pressing it on a board placed on the ground.

Where does it sink in furthest?

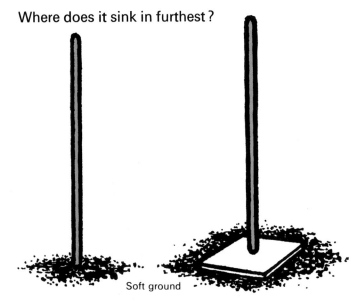

Soft ground

78

Building a wall

Watch the bricklayer at work. How many bricks does he lay in an hour?

How does he arrange his bricks? What other patterns of bricks can children find? How many different kinds of bricks can he show the children? They might be allowed to take one brick of each sort back to school.

Are the bricks all the same size?

How heavy are they?

Do they have markings on them?

What colours are they?

Do they have different textures?

Many children would probably like to build their own wall back at school from wooden blocks, shoeboxes or ideally from real bricks and cement.

Much of the value of such a visit lies in the observations the children, almost unconsciously, make. They will probably be surprised that there is a cavity in the wall; they will note that door and window frames are put in place and the wall then built around them, that an air-brick is placed for ventilation and that a damp course is put in to prevent water rising up the wall.

Stand a brick in a bowl of water back at school and watch the water rise up it.

Stand another brick on top of it, as shown, and see if water will pass into it.

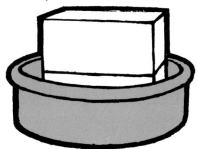

Try placing materials between two bricks to prevent water passing from one to the other. Can you get a piece of real damp course material from the building site?

How much does a brick weigh before and after soaking in water?

Materials

What materials are used on the site? Sand, cement, chippings, bricks, breeze blocks, tiles, slates, wood, glass (both translucent and transparent), roofing felt, metals, putty can all be collected for school. What shapes and textures do they have?

Where, for example, are all the places metals are used on the site? Children may suggest drainpipes, guttering, window frames, door handles, drain covers, metal stays in the wall (if they watched the bricklayer), nails and so on. Are all the metals painted? Why are some painted?

Workmen

Talking to workmen is fun. How are they dressed? Do they have patches on their trousers? Why do we need to put patches on clothes? (See page 70.) What are their boots like? Why do they have thick rubber soles or hob-nails in them? (See page 70.)

Do the men wear overalls? What sort of fabric are they made from? Perhaps a child can bring an old piece of overall to school so that children can stretch it and find out how tough it is. This might lead to making a collection of fabrics and seeing how strong they are.

Do any of the men wear special overalls? Talk to the carpenter. What sort of pocket does he keep his rule in? How does his rule open and shut?

Tools and machines

What tools are used on the site? These will vary but try and see some of the tools used by the general labourer, the carpenter, the glazier, the bricklayer, the plumber, the painter, the plasterer and the tiler. If possible see what they are used for. Posing questions may help. How does the bricklayer test that his wall is vertical? How does he carry bricks up a ladder? Make a class collection of tools brought from home.

Where are machines used on the site? Perhaps a concrete mixer, a crane, a simple pulley, a compressor and a drill. Make models of these.

Where do the workmen use water? Its uses may vary from mixing cement to making tea.

What do lorries bring to the site and what do they take away?

Noise
Of course, a building site has sounds all of its own (see page 31).

A mock building site
At school children might make their own building site. Large boxes placed together or a rostrum help to give two different levels.

'Bricks' (wooden blocks, shoeboxes) can be wheeled up a plank.

What differences do you feel between pushing the wheelbarrow on the floor and up the plank?

If it is possible increase or decrease the slope of the plank. Does this make a difference?

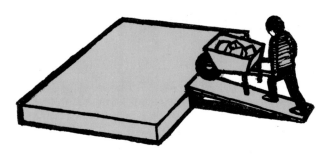

The traditional three-sided Wendy house might be put on the rostrum and a wall built across the front with shoeboxes.

How do the children arrange their bricks?

Can they improvise a doorway and a window?

Is it best to build these first and place the bricks around them?

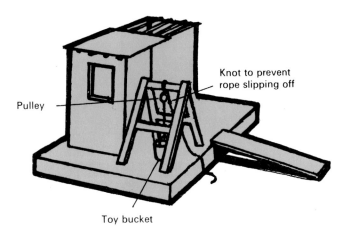

Knot to prevent rope slipping off

Pulley

Toy bucket

Can you make a roof? At its simplest this might just be joists, made from bamboo rods or thin strips of wood, placed across the Wendy house with cartridge paper resting on them.

With a suitable support such as an old beam, or part of the PE apparatus, or an easel, it is possible to hang a pulley.

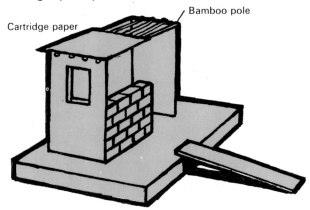

Cartridge paper

Bamboo pole

Often schools possess a little workbench and this can be moved nearby to act as the site carpenter's bench—and, of course, lists of all the tools can be drawn up and placed near it.

Imitative play is important in the children's world. Having visited a building site they will come up with lots of ideas of their own and perhaps inveigle their fathers into loaning bits and pieces for their 'site'.

Looking at one another

Children are always interested in themselves. An endless number of statistics can be gathered from the class and often these can be graphed.

What is the total number of children?

How many boys? How many girls?

How many stay for lunch?

How many wear jumpers? How many wear shirts?

How many brothers and sisters do they have?

How many people live in their house?

How many pets do they have?

When are the children's birthdays?

Length
Who is the tallest in the class? What ways can the children find of measuring the height of each child?

Who has the longest hand? Draw round them to find out. Draw round feet on to newspaper and cut them out. Who has the longest newspaper foot?

Weight
What weight is each child in the class? What were their birth weights? Let them take a piece of paper home to write it down on—it's the sort of statistic mothers always remember.

Silhouettes
Join some newspapers or sugar paper together and let children lie out on them so that their silhouettes can be drawn. Cut out the shape. Can they work out who has got the largest silhouette? In many cases it will be obvious. If the silhouette is drawn on squared paper children need only count the squares to arrive at an answer.

Another method might be to place small tiles or snap cards over the silhouette and count how many of these are needed to cover it.

Hands and feet
Draw round these and obtain silhouettes. They might stretch their thumb and little finger as far apart as possible when drawing round their hand in order to obtain a span.

Who has the largest span?

How many spans long is the classroom?

Look at fingerprints and thumbprints. (Use a magnifier.) Are they all different? What are the children's shoe sizes? Graph them.

Senses
There is much work that can be done on these. See 'Eyes', page 71; 'Ears', page 38; 'Taste', page 59; 'Smell', page 58.

Hair
What colours? Who has the longest? How strong is hair?

One end of a hair might be tied to a nail and the other end to a toy bucket. This demands the greatest dexterity.

How many washers or nails can be put in the bucket before the hair strand snaps?

Of course such considerations often lead elsewhere. What other animals have hair?

Real hair will curl if pulled under a pencil several times.

Do the children's dolls have real or artificial hair?

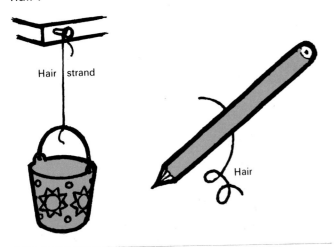

Hair strand

Hair

Looking at a piece of waste ground

Many waste sites are too large for an infant class to tackle and it is therefore wise to decide on a small area to investigate. If this has physical boundaries so much the better.

Materials
A start might be made by collecting all the non-living things—stones, pebbles, bones, plastics, wood, metal, bricks, tiles, tin cans and so on. What ways can children find of sorting these and what tests can they devise to find out more about them? (See 'Comparing things', page 40.)

Plants
What plants are present? How many are in flower? Some children might like to concentrate on a single plant. How tall is it? How deep are its roots? Is it difficult or easy to pull from the soil?

How many flowers does it have? How many fruits? How many seeds?

Shapes of plants, and of parts of plants, are interesting. Does the plant have round or square stems or what? What shape are the leaves?

Leaves are often arranged in a definite pattern. Sometimes they are opposite one another, sometimes alternate, sometimes in a spiral up the stem. What leaf arrangements can children find?

If two leaves are placed on top of one another, do they ever fit exactly? Can you tell by feel alone which is the top and which is the bottom of a leaf?

Colouring varies enormously, even within a single plant. What colours or shades of colour can the children find on the plants they study? What about the colour of the plant in relation to its background—is it easy or difficult to pick out?

Which flowers have a smell? Closing their eyes often helps children to concentrate more closely on this aspect. Do not forget that parts of plants other than flowers may give a smell, rub leaves or parts of leaves together. Some plants spread their odour over a wide area and some children might be interested in estimating how far they can go from a group of flowers before they can no longer smell them.

Many plants have a single flower at the tip of a stem but other arrangements prevail, especially where a plant bears many flowers. What arrangements can children discover? Often plants such as hogweed have groupings of very tiny flowers—how are these arranged?

Which plant is most numerous? Does this plant cover the largest area. Note the space occupied by plants and the directions they spread out.

Many plants have special features which are worth looking at such as thorns and tendrils and it is worth noting how leaves, fruits and seeds are attached to the plant. Some plants sting.

Animals

A large number of animals will turn up. Their shape, movement, methods of feeding and taking in air (where this can be seen), reproduction and habits can be studied as outlined on pages 62-65.

Children can also list the places they find the animals and sometimes set up temporary homes for them in the classroom.

Terrain

What about the nature of the ground ? Where do you find slopes, puddles, paths and worn grass ?

Other areas

There are many areas worth considering with infants. Just think what could come from a visit to a :

hole in the road	dairy
farm	fire station
docks	rocky shore
railway station	park

Rainy day things

Wet things

Wet materials

Begin by wetting fabrics. Try gaberdine, PVC, leather, linen, nylon, cotton and so on. What words can children find to describe these fabrics when dry and when wet?

Words like absorbent, waterproof, soggy and so on will probably fit well into this context. Make a list of fabrics that will absorb water easily and another list of those that will not. Which fabrics will let water through?

Try timing the passage of a tablespoonful of water through each fabric.

Does it make a difference if you start with the material wet?

Which fabrics do children think will be best for a rainy day? What sort of clothes do they wear on a rainy day?

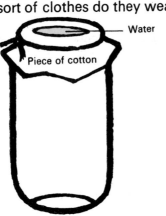

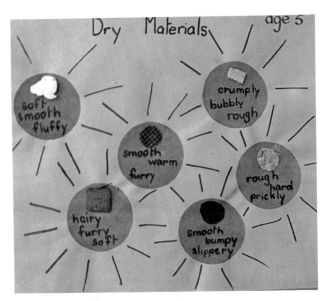

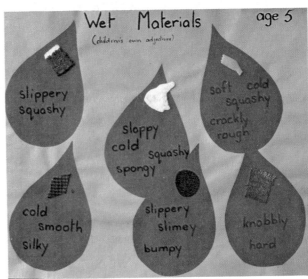

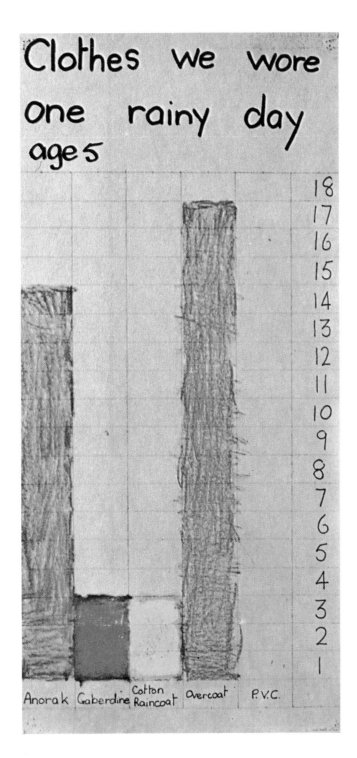

Clothes we wore one rainy day age 5

18 17 16 15 14 13 12 11 10 9 8 7 6 5 4 3 2 1

Anorak   Gaberdine   Cotton Raincoat   Overcoat   P.V.C.

Where to dry Clothes age 5

1. radiator
2. wind
3. sun
4. indoors
5. in a heap

Drying conditions
How can you dry wet fabrics?

Will some fabrics dry faster than others? Does the size of the piece of material you use matter? Does it matter *where* you dry the fabrics?

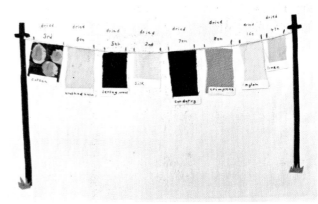

Which fabric dries first? The children's report is given on the next page

We weighed all the materials dry. and then we weighed them wet. when we weighed the crimplene wet 58 bottle tops had to be put on. The nylon dried first. and the silk dried second Lorraine wetted them and April put them on the scales Katrina put the bottle tops on the scales and I counted how many bottle tops had to be put and Ann wrote the number on a piece of paper and that is how we weighed our materials.

We wondered what would happen f our coats were all reddy vet and we had to go out in the rain so we made our materials wet first. Then we added two tea-spoon-full of vater and watched them. The water soaked through and the materials except one which vas the plastic one.

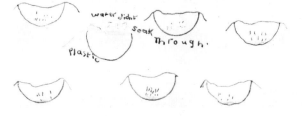

Which material will water pass through?

How would you dry a wet umbrella ? Try rubbing a small area. Try turning it slowly above a radiator. Can you think of any better methods ?

Which days will be best for drying things ?

Drying effect of the sun
Note the drying effect of the sun after rain. Why does the playground steam after a thunderstorm ?

Mark the outline of a puddle with chalk at the start of morning school and re-mark it at frequent intervals. How does the rate of drying compare on sunny and cloudy days ? Many infants think puddle water just sinks into the ground. It is an area ripe for gathering experience. Try leaving a jar of water on the window-sill and marking the daily water level with a wax crayon. What happens to water in a similar jar but having a tight-fitting lid ?

Weighing wet things
What does a piece of material weigh before and after wetting ? Can children think out ways of weighing the water ?

If they are not using standard weights they might weigh the material against nails, or washers or some other arbitrary unit. They might investigate how the increase in weight alters as the *amount* of material alters. How much does a wet blanket weigh ? How much does it weigh after drying on a clothes line ? There is a surprising difference.

Retrieving and soaking up water
How can water be retrieved from fabrics ? Try wringing, squeezing, shaking, pounding.

Which fabrics soak up puddles of water most quickly ? Again children should be encouraged to suggest their own such as a cotton handkerchief, a woollen jumper, a sponge and then try them out.

Fabrics can also be hung with their ends dipping in water to see which fabric takes up water the fastest.

This might be adapted as a game.

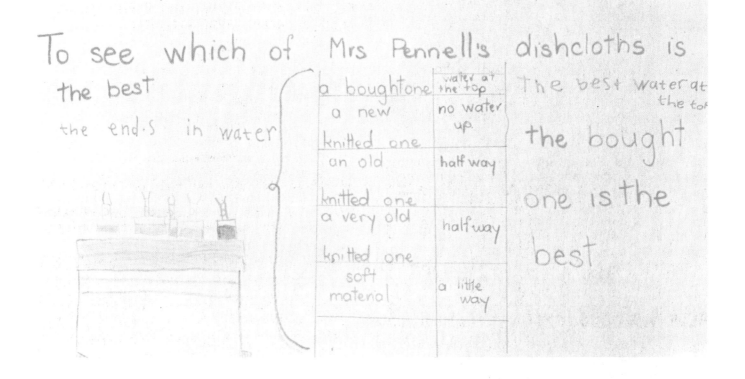

To see which of Mrs Pennell's dishcloths is the best

the ends in water

a bought one	water at the top
a new knitted one	no water up.
an old knitted one	half way
a very old knitted one	half way
knitted one soft material	a little way

The best water at the top the bought one is the best

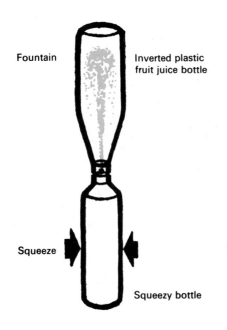

Fountain

Inverted plastic fruit juice bottle

Squeeze

Squeezy bottle

Shrinking
Some fabrics shrink in water. It is useful to have two similar-sized pieces of such fabric, one of which is soaked and allowed to dry. This the children can then compare with the piece which did not receive this treatment. A number of fabrics are a different shade of colour when wet, others lose their dye in water; both these are useful talking points.

Favourite forms of water
What are the children's favourite forms of water? One class said ice, water pistol fuel, lollipops, waterfalls, puddles, fire-engine water and fountains.

Make a fountain.

Rain

Measuring rainfall
Rain can be collected in a tin. It is an easy matter to transfer this to an Alka-Seltzer tube each day and end up with a ready-made histogram of the weekly rainfall.

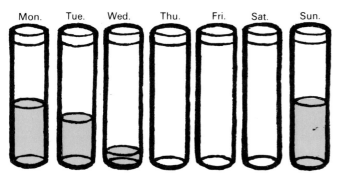

The height of the water in each tube might be recorded on a block graph (a piece of paper placed behind the tubes with the water level marked in), and records kept for as long as the children's interest lasts.

Where does water come from?
Rain, of course, but some children will suggest taps. Where are all the taps in the school? It may be possible to trace some of the water pipes.

List all the uses of water: drinking, washing, cooking, making tea, flushing the toilet.

Where does the water go after it has rained? Look at the guttering, drainpipes and drains.

Drops of water
Raindrops move down the windowpane. Which move fastest? Where else can children find drops of water? Children might suggest drops in a washbasin or dew on the grass. Are all drops the same size?

Feel drops of water.

Put a drop of water on the end of one finger and bring your thumb gently up against it.

What happens if you slowly pull your finger away?

What is the smallest drop of water you can make? Can you make up ways of making 'drops'? Try

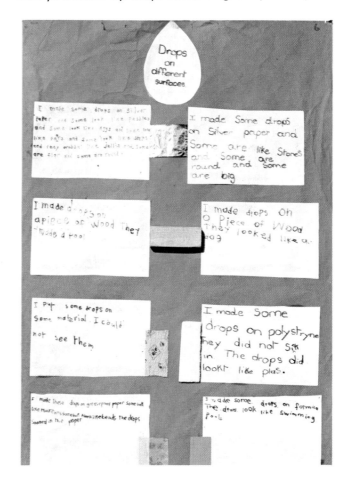

fingers, a pencil or a piece of wood, a drinking straw or a medicine dropper. What else can you think of to try?

What do drops look like on different surfaces such as a wood block, a polished table top, a piece of cloth, silver paper off a chocolate bar, or some greaseproof paper? In the rounding off of the water surface in this way children are gaining more and more experience of a phenomenon that the scientist calls surface tension.

Which surfaces do drops travel along most quickly? Gently tip a Formica table top up, or let a drop run along a tilted wood block or over a tilted piece of polystyrene. Have drop races with one another. What is left when the drop has evaporated?

Lightning, thunder and rainbows
Count the seconds between a lightning stroke and the resultant thunder. This gives an indication of how near the lightning is. Many children frightened by thunder may be reassured if they play a game in which they 'time' a storm as it approaches, passes overhead and recedes.

Often after a storm a rainbow appears. Look for rainbows in puddles, at the edge of an aquarium or perhaps one formed by the sunlight striking through the window. Try making your own rainbow by pouring oil on to the surface of water in a bucket and setting this out in the sunshine.

Water and soil

Wet soil
Collect wet soil. How long does it take to dry? Dry some soil thoroughly. What colour is it? Has it changed in texture?

Make some bricks with damp soil.

Try making small bricks with damp sand, mud or a wet mixture of cement and sand.

Soil and water
Different quantities of soils can be stirred in the same amount of water. How long does each take to settle? What does the soil look like when it has settled? Children may notice that the coarser material in the soil settles most quickly followed by fine sand and silt.

How can the soil be got back from the water? Children who have been investigating the drying effect of the sun might suggest evaporation. Others might suggest a strainer or a piece of muslin (see page 57).

Games for rainy days

Guessing games
What is in the bag?
A series of shoe-bags, each containing a different object, can be set out on a table. Include some objects with a distinctive texture and shape, eg a coconut, piece of velvet, pineapple, cucumber. Children have to guess what is in each bag by touch alone.

The bags arouse much curiosity and speculation —it is interesting to include some objects that make a noise. Experiences involving shape, size, hardness, weight and texture arise naturally from this game.

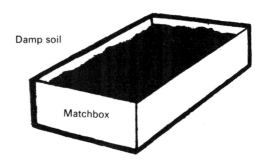

Damp soil

Matchbox

What is in the tin?

A child might collect a series of small objects such as a rubber, a paper-clip, a marble, a pencil and a crayon and put these, one at a time, into a tin with a close-fitting lid. He could then ask his friends to guess what is in the tin without opening it. By listening and feeling as he tumbles the object the child begins to get clues about its size, shape and weight and may eventually guess what it is.

What reactions do children give to a liquid inside the tin?

Snap cards

What is in my pocket?

Generally a game for boys. One boy empties his pocket of all objects bar one. Holding this object in his pocket he gives clues about it to a group of boys around him. He will have to talk about size, shape, colour, texture and hardness. The first individual to guess the object gets the next turn to choose an object from his pocket.

Snap

Make some snap cards using different shapes and colours. Children can call snap when the same shape or colour appear together.

No thumbs

Man has an opposable thumb (ie it approaches the fingers across the palm) which enables him to grasp objects. Many children will have noticed that a squirrel, for example, when feeding on a nut grasps it with both paws.

How useful is a thumb? Let children try picking up small objects without using a thumb. Can they think of other tasks? Turning pages, buttoning a coat, using scissors, tying shoe-laces, drinking from a cup are all much more difficult, if not impossible, without thumbs.

Can children think of any other animals that use thumbs?

Wintry things

Winter is a time when we tend to neglect or ignore the outdoor environment. It need not be for there is still much to see and discuss.

Sleepers and non-sleepers

Hibernation is a common topic in infant class-rooms; often a picture or frieze of the winter scene drawn by children will show an animal fast asleep in a hollow tree trunk. The bare winter landscape as well as the almost lack of sound tend to convey an impression of dormancy, of there being nothing around. Is this really so?

Look under large stones, in piles of rubbish and in rotting logs, you will almost certainly find woodlice, spiders, beetles and snails. Break open the hollow stems of plants that have died away, such as the lupin, there will probably be some insects there.

Watch for grey squirrels and rabbits which do not hibernate, and if possible observe their movement and general habits for this is one of the best times of year to see them clearly. Animals that do hibernate or at least sleep for long periods are frogs, newts, snakes, many fish, hedgehogs, badgers, bats and mice.

Many birds, especially those that feed on insects, have migrated. Watch for the birds that are left for they often crowd near houses to pick up scraps put out for them. This is an especially good time to put out a bird-table at school and observe the birds that visit it. Look at their general characteristics, movement and habits (see pages 62-65). How well do they merge with their background? Look at blackbirds, thrushes and sparrows for their camouflage is good. How well do other animals blend with their surroundings? Can you camouflage an egg-box to merge with the top of a table or the school field?

Plants, of course, exist as seeds, bulbs, corms, tubers and rhizomes (many with a large food store) over the winter. Do not forget to look from time to time at the bowl containing crocuses so that you see the first shoots appearing. Get some of the special glass containers for growing hyacinths so that children can see the first roots appearing as well as the shoots.

Watch for the common weeds such as groundsel, shepherd's purse and dandelion, and flowers such as primroses, crocuses and hazel which appear early in the year.

Snow and ice

The first snow with its soft, fluffy texture usually generates much enthusiasm. Children pack it together to make snowballs. Where else can they find compacted snow? Perhaps under the heels of shoes or where cars have been parked in a corner of the school grounds.

Is the depth of snow different in different places?

Why should this be so?

What happens if you add water to snow?

What makes snow melt?

What does snow taste like?

Bring some snow into school in a large tin and fill a jam jar with it. How much water comes from it when it has melted? Weigh a jam jar full of snow, weigh it when the snow has melted. Is there a difference?

Making a snowman
Children usually begin by rolling a small ball of snow around on the playground where the ability of snow to form compact masses becomes more and more apparent as the ball increases in size.

What height is the snowman?   What diameter?

How many cones and buttons do you need for his nose and eyes?

How long does he take to melt?

Deborah wrote:

'I made a snowman with my brother. It had a fat head and a thin body and the head kept falling off, so we got a bottle of water and poured the water in the crack and the snowman's head stuck on. We left the shampoo bottle with water in on the coal bunker. This morning the bottle had broken and cracked into pieces. The water wasn't in but a block of ice was.'

Snowflakes
Snowflakes usually melt before children can look at them with a magnifier and it is necessary to look at pictures. Note the variety and how they always form a six-pointed star. Symmetry shows up well here (see pages 29 and 30).

Make some snowflake patterns by cutting out a circle from paper (draw round a large tin lid), fold it in six and cut pieces from it. These look quite effective displayed against black paper, and there is no reason why children should not learn that snowflakes are also called crystals. Why not look at sugar crystals as well?

Footprints
Footprints show up well in snow (see page 52). Make some walking footprints, running footprints, hopping footprints. Can your friends guess which are which? Look for animal footprints. Can you distinguish between those caused by a walking bird and those caused by a hopping bird? What direction are the prints going in? Where do they lead? Try to draw the shapes of the prints.

Tobogganing
Of course this is fun. Time the toboggan on each journey over a sloping playground or down a gently inclined bank. Who travels most quickly? Is it not fair to have a fixed starting and a fixed finishing point? How long is the track?

Ice
Looking and feeling
Look at ice, note the form it takes as icicles, feathery patterns on the windowpanes, frost on the grass. How does ice feel? How does it taste? Watch as it forms in puddles, bird baths and ponds. Note how there is often water under the ice surface and talk about the fish that live there and how difficult it is for many water birds to get food.

Melting

Collect some ice in a plastic bag. Put pieces in different jam jars around the classroom. Where does it melt most quickly? Why is this? Here again is a chance to develop vocabulary for ice is a *solid* which turns to a *liquid*. Where else can children think of this happening?

Ice lollies

Make some ice lollies in the school refrigerator. What can you think of to flavour them with? (See page 59.)

Fill the compartments in the ice-box exactly to the top with the ice lolly mixture. What happens to it when it has frozen? How long does an ice cube take to melt? In what ways can an ice cube be made to melt faster than it does in air? Who can devise the best way to preserve an ice cube?

What happens to an ice cube placed in water? How much of it is below the water surface? This may lead to talking about icebergs and why they are a danger to shipping. Some children might be interested in talking about food preservation. In what ways can food be preserved? Set up a display of preserved food.

Keeping warm

This is a problem for all animals. Keeping ourselves warm is discussed on page 67, but don't forget to discuss how sheep develop shaggy coats, birds fluff out their feathers and even the fur of domestic pets gets thicker.

How is the school kept warm? If possible visit the boiler-house and let the caretaker show the children how the boiler is fired.

Can you trace the pipes from the boiler-house around the school? Are any of them lagged? Children who have experienced how water can expand as it changes to ice, for example in making their ice lollies, may begin to appreciate the need for such lagging.

What other ways of heating a building are there? Discuss how the children heat their own homes and let them cut and mount different pictures from magazines showing this.

Materials and equipment

Basic everyday materials that can be collected

Squeezy bottles, jam jars, jugs, plastic containers (all shapes and sizes), bottles, tins, wood, rocks and pebbles, yoghurt and cream cartons, boxes, bricks, matchboxes, cartons, cardboard, paper, fabrics, bottle tops, corks, toilet and kitchen roll centres, cotton reels, tin lids, wire, newspaper, tea chests, nuts and bolts, old clocks (to take to pieces), locks and keys, buttons, beads, shells, sand, feathers, Meccano and nylon stockings.

Basic everyday materials that can be bought

Plastic buckets, medicine droppers, spoons, funnels, hose-pipe, watering cans, sieves, rubber tubing, sponges, mirrors, bowls, bubble pipes, drinking straws, sand, polythene bags, Plasticine, gauze, cotton, building bricks (all shapes and sizes), Meccano, Dinky cars, string, seeds, candles, blotting paper, silver paper, plaster of Paris, coloured gummed paper, torches, muslin, timers, elastic bands, plastic sandwich boxes and magnifiers.

A workbench

A workbench is a very useful item, especially if fitted with a vice. It is also useful to have a hammer, tenon saw, hand-drill and bits, bradawl, screwdrivers, nails, screws, glue, sand-paper, emery paper, paint, varnish and brushes.

Additional items

Most of the following items can be obtained from any apparatus suppliers, for example,

E. J. Arnold & Son Limited, Butterley Street, Leeds 10
Griffin & George Limited, Ealing Road, Alperton, Wembley
Philip Harris, Ludgate Hill, Birmingham 3

Colour paddles, kaleidoscopes, lenses, magnifying sheet (Fresnel biprism principle), mirrors, pulleys, stethoscope, transparent acetate sheet (coloured), tubing, plastic and rubber.

Large Woolworth's stores, cycle shops and iron-mongers usually hold stocks of :

Batteries 4·5 V	Electric bell
Bulb-holders	Single-strand bell wire
Bulbs 3·5 V	

Electric motors and propellors can be obtained from most model shops.

Objectives for children learning science
Guide lines to keep in mind

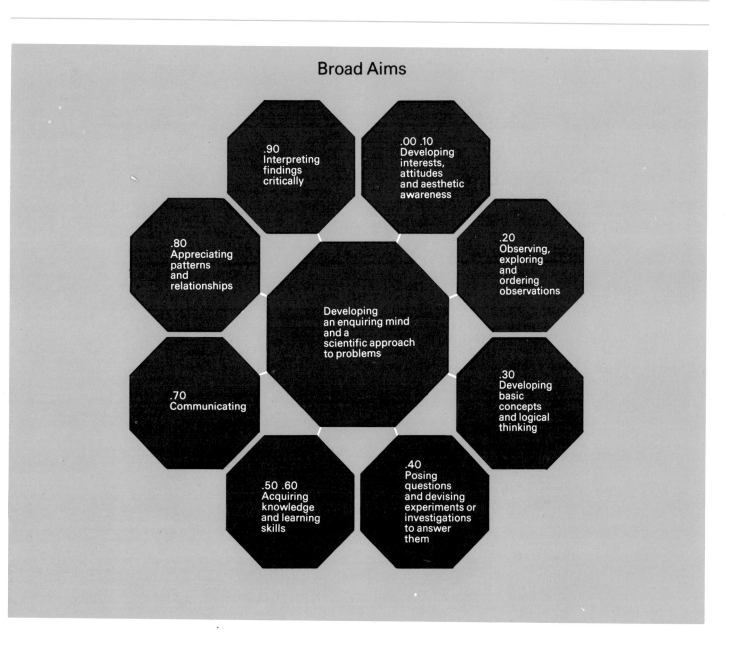

Broad Aims

.90 Interpreting findings critically

.00 .10 Developing interests, attitudes and aesthetic awareness

.80 Appreciating patterns and relationships

.20 Observing, exploring and ordering observations

Developing an enquiring mind and a scientific approach to problems

.70 Communicating

.30 Developing basic concepts and logical thinking

.50 .60 Acquiring knowledge and learning skills

.40 Posing questions and devising experiments or investigations to answer them

What we mean by Stage 1, Stage 2 and Stage 3

Attitudes, interests and aesthetic awareness

.00/.10

Stage 1
Transition from intuition to concrete operations. Infants generally.

The characteristics of thought among infant children differ in important respects from those of children over the age of about seven years. Infant thought has been described as 'intuitive' by Piaget; it is closely associated with physical action and is dominated by immediate observation. Generally, the infant is not able to think about or imagine the consequences of an action unless he has actually carried it out, nor is he yet likely to draw logical conclusions from his experiences. At this early stage the objectives are those concerned with active exploration of the immediate environment and the development of ability to discuss and communicate effectively: they relate to the kind of activities that are appropriate to these very young children, and which form an introduction to ways of exploring and of ordering observations.

1.01 Willingness to ask questions
1.02 Willingness to handle both living and non-living material.
1.03 Sensitivity to the need for giving proper care to living things.
1.04 Enjoyment in using all the senses for exploring and discriminating.
1.05 Willingness to collect material for observation or investigation.

Concrete operations. Early stage.

In this Stage, children are developing the ability to manipulate things mentally. At first this ability is limited to objects and materials that can be manipulated concretely, and even then only in a restricted way. The objectives here are concerned with developing these mental operations through exploration of concrete objects and materials—that is to say, objects and materials which, as physical things, have meaning for the child. Since older children, and even adults, prefer an introduction to new ideas and problems through concrete example and physical exploration, these objectives are suitable for all children, whatever their age, who are being introduced to certain science activities for the first time.

1.06 Desire to find out things for oneself.
1.07 Willing participation in group work.
1.08 Willing compliance with safety regulations in handling tools and equipment.
1.09 Appreciation of the need to learn the meaning of new words and to use them correctly.

Stage 2
Concrete operations. Later stage.

In this Stage, a continuation of what Piaget calls the stage of concrete operations, the mental manipulations are becoming more varied and powerful. The developing ability to handle variables—for example, in dealing with multiple classification—means that problems can be solved in more ordered and quantitative ways than was previously possible. The objectives begin to be more specific to the exploration of the scientific aspects of the environment rather than to general experience, as previously. These objectives are developments of those of Stage 1 and depend on them for a foundation. They are those thought of as being appropriate for all children who have progressed from Stage 1 and not merely for nine- to eleven-year-olds.

2.01 Willingness to co-operate with others in science activities.
2.02 Willingness to observe objectively.
2.03 Appreciation of the reasons for safety regulations.
2.04 Enjoyment in examining ambiguity in the use of words.
2.05 Interest in choosing suitable means of expressing results and observations.
2.06 Willingness to assume responsibility for the proper care of living things.
2.07 Willingness to examine critically the results of their own and others' work.
2.08 Preference for putting ideas to test before accepting or rejecting them.
2.09 Appreciation that approximate methods of comparison may be more appropriate than careful measurements.

Stage 3
Transition to stage of abstract thinking.

This is the Stage in which, for some children, the ability to think about abstractions is developing. When this development is complete their thought is capable of dealing with the possible and hypothetical, and is not tied to the concrete and to the here and now. It may take place between eleven and thirteen for some able children, for some children it may happen later, and for others it may never occur. The objectives of this stage are ones which involve development of ability to use hypothetical reasoning and to separate and combine variables in a systematic way. They are appropriate to those who have achieved most of the Stage 2 objectives and who now show signs of ability to manipulate mentally ideas and propositions.

3.01 Acceptance of responsibility for their own and others' safety in experiments.
3.02 Preference for using words correctly.
3.03 Commitment to the idea of physical cause and effect.
3.04 Recognition of the need to standardise measurements.
3.05 Willingness to examine evidence critically.
3.06 Willingness to consider beforehand the usefulness of the results from a possible experiment.
3.07 Preference for choosing the most appropriate means of expressing results or observations.
3.08 Recognition of the need to acquire new skills.
3.09 Willingness to consider the role of science in everyday life.

Attitudes, interests and aesthetic awareness

.00/.10

1.11 Awareness that there are various ways of testing out ideas and making observations.
1.12 Interest in comparing and classifying living or non-living things.
1.13 Enjoyment in comparing measurements with estimates.
1.14 Awareness that there are various ways of expressing results and observations.
1.15 Willingness to wait and to keep records in order to observe change in things.
1.16 Enjoyment in exploring the variety of living things in the environment.
1.17 Interest in discussing and comparing the aesthetic qualities of materials.

2.11 Enjoyment in developing methods for solving problems or testing ideas.
2.12 Appreciation of the part that aesthetic qualities of materials play in determining their use.
2.13 Interest in the way discoveries were made in the past.

3.11 Appreciation of the main principles in the care of living things.
3.12 Willingness to extend methods used in science activities to other fields of experience.

Observing, exploring and ordering observations

.20

1.21 Appreciation of the variety of living things and materials in the environment.
1.22 Awareness of changes which take place as time passes.
1.23 Recognition of common shapes—square, circle, triangle.
1.24 Recognition of regularity in patterns.
1.25 Ability to group things consistently according to chosen or given criteria.

1.26 Awareness of the structure and form of living things.
1.27 Awareness of change of living things and non-living materials.
1.28 Recognition of the action of force
1.29 Ability to group living and non-living things by observable attributes.
1.29a Ability to distinguish regularity in events and motion.

2.21 Awareness of internal structure in living and non-living things.
2.22 Ability to construct and use keys for identification.
2.23 Recognition of similar and congruent shapes.
2.24 Awareness of symmetry in shapes and structures.
2.25 Ability to classify living things and non-living materials in different ways.
2.26 Ability to visualise objects from different angles and the shape of cross-sections.

3.21 Appreciation that classification criteria are arbitrary.
3.22 Ability to distinguish observations which are relevant to the solution of a problem from those which are not.
3.23 Ability to estimate the order of magnitude of physical quantities.

	Developing basic concepts and logical thinking .30	**Posing questions and devising experiments or investigations to answer them** .40
Stage 1 Transition from intuition to concrete operations. Infants generally.	*1.31* Awareness of the meaning of words which describe various types of quantity. *1.32* Appreciation that things which are different may have features in common.	*1.41* Ability to find answers to simple problems by investigation. *1.42* Ability to make comparisons in terms of one property or variable.
Concrete operations. Early stage.	*1.33* Ability to predict the effect of certain changes through observation of similar changes. *1.34* Formation of the notions of the horizontal and the vertical. *1.35* Development of concepts of conservation of length and substance. *1.36* Awareness of the meaning of speed and of its relation to distance covered.	*1.43* Appreciation of the need for measurement. *1.44* Awareness that more than one variable may be involved in a particular change.
Stage 2 Concrete operations. Later stage.	*2.31* Appreciation of measurement as division into regular parts and repeated comparison with a unit. *2.32* Appreciation that comparisons can be made indirectly by use of an intermediary. *2.33* Development of concepts of conservation of weight, area and volume. *2.34* Appreciation of weight as a downward force. *2.35* Understanding of the speed, time, distance relation.	*2.41* Ability to frame questions likely to be answered through investigations. *2.42* Ability to investigate variables and to discover effective ones. *2.43* Appreciation of the need to control variables and use controls in investigations. *2.44* Ability to choose and use either arbitrary or standard units of measurement as appropriate. *2.45* Ability to select a suitable degree of approximation and work to it. *2.46* Ability to use representational models for investigating problems or relationships.
Stage 3 Transition to stage of abstract thinking.	*3.31* Familiarity with relationships involving velocity, distance, time, acceleration. *3.32* Ability to separate, exclude or combine variables in approaching problems. *3.33* Ability to formulate hypotheses not dependent upon direct observation. *3.34* Ability to extend reasoning beyond the actual to the possible. *3.35* Ability to distinguish a logically sound proof from others less sound.	*3.41* Attempting to identify the essential steps in approaching a problem scientifically. *3.42* Ability to design experiments with effective controls for testing hypotheses. *3.43* Ability to visualise a hypothetical situation as a useful simplification of actual observations. *3.44* Ability to construct scale models for investigation and to appreciate implications of changing the scale.

100

Acquiring knowledge and learning skills

.50/.60

1.51 Ability to discriminate between different materials.
1.52 Awareness of the characteristics of living things.
1.53 Awareness of properties which materials can have.
1.54 Ability to use displayed reference material for identifying living and non-living things.

Acquiring knowledge and learning skills

.50/.60

1.55 Familiarity with sources of sound.
1.56 Awareness of sources of heat, light and electricity.
1.57 Knowledge that change can be produced in common substances.
1.58 Appreciation that ability to move or cause movement requires energy.
1.59 Knowledge of differences in properties between and within common groups of materials.

1.61 Appreciation of man's use of other living things and their products.
1.62 Awareness that man's way of life has changed through the ages.
1.63 Skill in manipulating tools and materials.
1.64 Development of techniques for handling living things correctly.
1.65 Ability to use books for supplementing ideas or information.

2.51 Knowledge of conditions which promote changes in living things and non-living materials.
2.52 Familiarity with a wide range of forces and of ways in which they can be changed.
2.53 Knowledge of sources and simple properties of common forms of energy.
2.54 Knowledge of the origins of common materials.
2.55 Awareness of some discoveries and inventions by famous scientists.
2.56 Knowledge of ways to investigate and measure properties of living things and non-living materials.
2.57 Awareness of changes in the design of measuring instruments and tools during man's history.
2.58 Skill in devising and constructing simple apparatus.
2.59 Ability to select relevant information from books or other reference material.

3.51 Knowledge that chemical change results from interaction.
3.52 Knowledge that energy can be stored and converted in various ways.
3.53 Awareness of the universal nature of gravity.
3.54 Knowledge of the main constituents and variations in the composition of soil and of the earth.
3.55 Knowledge that properties of matter can be explained by reference to its particulate nature.
3.56 Knowledge of certain properties of heat, light, sound, electrical, mechanical and chemical energy.
3.57 Knowledge of a wide range of living organisms.
3.58 Development of the concept of an internal environment.
3.59 Knowledge of the nature and variations in basic life processes.

3.61 Appreciation of levels of organisation in living things.
3.62 Appreciation of the significance of the work and ideas of some famous scientists.
3.63 Ability to apply relevant knowledge without help of contextual cues.
3.64 Ability to use scientific equipment and instruments for extending the range of human senses.

Communicating	Appreciating patterns and relationships
.70	**.80**

Stage 1
Transition from
intuition to
concrete
operations.
Infants
generally.

Communicating	Appreciating patterns and relationships
1.71 Ability to use new words appropriately.	*1.81* Awareness of cause-effect relationships.
1.72 Ability to record events in their sequences.	
1.73 Ability to discuss and record impressions of living and non-living things in the environment.	
1.74 Ability to use representational symbols for recording information on charts or block graphs.	

Concrete
operations.
Early stage.

Communicating	Appreciating patterns and relationships
1.75 Ability to tabulate information and use tables.	*1.82* Development of a concept of environment.
1.76 Familiarity with names of living things and non-living materials.	*1.83* Formation of a broad idea of variation in living things.
1.77 Ability to record impressions by making models, painting or drawing.	*1.84* Awareness of seasonal changes in living things.
	1.85 Awareness of differences in physical conditions between different parts of the Earth.

Stage 2
Concrete
operations.
Later stage.

Communicating	Appreciating patterns and relationships
2.71 Ability to use non-representational symbols in plans, charts, etc.	*2.81* Awareness of sequences of change in natural phenomena.
2.72 Ability to interpret observations in terms of trends and rates of change.	*2.82* Awareness of structure-function relationship in parts of living things.
2.73 Ability to use histograms and other simple graphical forms for communicating data.	*2.83* Appreciation of interdependence among living things.
2.74 Ability to construct models as a means of recording observations.	*2.84* Awareness of the impact of man's activities on other living things.
	2.85 Awareness of the changes in the physical environment brought about by man's activity.
	2.86 Appreciation of the relationships of parts and wholes.

Stage 3
Transition to
stage of
abstract
thinking.

Communicating	Appreciating patterns and relationships
3.71 Ability to select the graphical form most appropriate to the information being recorded.	*3.81* Recognition that the ratio of volume to surface area is significant.
3.72 Ability to use three-dimensional models or graphs for recording results.	*3.82* Appreciation of the scale of the universe.
3.73 Ability to deduce information from graphs: from gradient, area, intercept.	*3.83* Understanding of the nature and significance of changes in living and non-living things.
3.74 Ability to use analogies to explain scientific ideas and theories.	*3.84* Recognition that energy has many forms and is conserved when it is changed from one form to another.
	3.85 Recognition of man's impact on living things— conservation, change, control.
	3.86 Appreciation of the social implications of man's changing use of materials, historical and contemporary.
	3.87 Appreciation of the social implications of research in science.
	3.88 Appreciation of the role of science in the changing pattern of provision for human needs.

Interpreting findings critically

.90

1.91 Awareness that the apparent size, shape and relationships of things depend on the position of the observer.

1.92 Appreciation that properties of materials influence their use.

2.91 Appreciation of adaptation to environment.
2.92 Appreciation of how the form and structure of materials relate to their function and properties.
2.93 Awareness that many factors need to be considered when choosing a material for a particular use.
2.94 Recognition of the role of chance in making measurements and experiments.

3.91 Ability to draw from observations conclusions that are unbiased by preconception.
3.92 Willingness to accept factual evidence despite perceptual contradictions
3.93 Awareness that the degree of accuracy of measurements has to be taken into account when results are interpreted.
3.94 Awareness that unstated assumptions can affect conclusions drawn from argument or experimental results.
3.95 Appreciation of the need to integrate findings into a simplifying generalisation.
3.96 Willingness to check that conclusions are consistent with further evidence.

These Stages we have chosen conform to modern ideas about children's learning. They conveniently describe for us the mental development of children between the ages of five and thirteen years, but it must be remembered that ALTHOUGH CHILDREN GO THROUGH THESE STAGES IN THE SAME ORDER THEY DO NOT GO THROUGH THEM AT THE SAME RATES.
SOME children achieve the later Stages at an early age.
SOME loiter in the early Stages for quite a time.
SOME never have the mental ability to develop to the later Stages.
ALL appear to be ragged in their movement from one Stage to another.
Our Stages, then, are not tied to chronological age, so in any one class of children there will be, almost certainly, some children at differing Stages of mental development.

Index

Illustration acknowledgements:

The publishers gratefully acknowledge the help given by the
following in supplying photographs on the pages indicated:

The Meteorological Office, 14
The Zoological Society of London, 91

South West Picture Agency, all other photographs

Line drawings by The Garden Studio: Anna Barnard

Cover design by Peter Gauld